Hikes Around
Fort Collins

Hikes Around Fort Collins

A Trail Guide

to Urban Hikes, Poudre Canyon, North Park, and Loveland

Melodie S. Edwards

WESTWINDS
PRESS®

THE PRUETT SERIES

© 2008 by Melodie S. Edwards

Interior photos by the author unless otherwise noted

Second edition

Library of Congress Cataloging-in-Publication Data
Edwards, Melodie S.
    Hikes Around Fort Collins: A Trail Guide to Urban Hikes, Poudre Canyon, North Park, and Loveland / Melodie S. Edwards.
        p. cm.
    Includes bibliographical references (p.) and index.

ISBN: 978-0-87108-952-6 (pbk.)
ISBN: 978-0-87108-991-5 (e-book)
ISBN: 978-0-87108-994-6 (hardbound)

    1. Hiking—Colorado—Guidebooks. 2. Cycling—Colorado—Guidebooks. 3. Trails—Colorado—Guidebooks. 4. Colorado—Guidebooks. I. Title
GV199.42.C6 E39 2001
917.8804'34—dc21   2001019354

WestWinds Press®
An imprint of Graphic Arts Books
P.O. Box 56118
Portland, OR 97238-6118
(503) 254-5591
www.graphicartsbooks.com

Design by Kay Turnbaugh
Cover photos: istock.com: © 2003 drflet; inset: istock.com: © 2006 John Upchurch

This book is dedicated to my dogs:
To the memory of Lucy, who passed on during the making of this book.
And to the happy arrival of Mora, who came into my life just in time to spend most of her puppyhood trailborne.
What would life on the soft path have been without you both?

Table of Contents

FORT COLLINS AREA TRAILS

POUDRE CANYON AREA TRAILS

NORTH PARK AREA TRAILS

PREFACE

A lot has happened in my life since I wrote the first edition of this guide. In the intervening seven years, I went on for a master's degree at the University of Michigan, brought twin girls into this world, and opened a used bookstore in Laramie, Wyoming. I am no longer the footloose outdoor zealot I was during the four years of intensive research I put into the original edition of this book. In writing this revised edition and returning to the lifestyle of the outdoor writer, I have been reminded what a great honor it is to take the reader by the hand and lead them into uncharted terrains.

It became clear to me that a new edition of the guide was necessary when I looked around Fort Collins and saw the astounding changes going on with the city and county open spaces of the area. With the construction of the **Blue Sky Trail**, a 9.75-mile trail spanning the foothills between Fort Collins and Loveland, and the completion of work on the **Coyote Ridge, Gateway Mountain Park** and **Eagle's Nest Rock** Trails, Fort Collins has become a hiking destination in its own right. For this reason, I also made the decision to alter the title of the book. Formerly titled *Trail Guide to Northern Colorado: Hiking and Skiing in Fort Collins, Poudre Canyon and North Park*, the new edition's focus on Fort Collins reflects the expansion of the "Around Town" sections of the book. The elimination of the ski sections of the old edition will also make the book a more packable and affordable piece of outdoor equipment.

I mentioned in my original "Preface" that I wrote the book while living in the small town of Walden, 100 miles west of Fort Collins, and that because it was easier for me to get to Red Canyon than it was to get to Horsetooth Rock the book inevitably emphasizes wild places. This time around, I revised the book while living in Laramie, Wyoming, and I believe my outsider eyes (although I graduated from high school and received my BA in Fort Collins) have allowed me to see what a wonderful gift the community of Fort Collins is giving itself through its city and county open space programs. Over the last couple decades I have watched the Front Range grow by leaps and bounds, and yet a person can now walk freely from the city limits of Fort Collins to the outskirts of Loveland with no worries but rattlesnakes.

But we mustn't take our eye off the long-term goal: I quoted Aldo Leopold once and I'll quote him again. "There are some who can live without wild things, and some who cannot." We live in the West because the horizons appear to go on forever, a constant reminder of a greater mystery beyond us. By walking tracelessly into that forever on foot, we acknowledge the essential value of wild things to a healthy society and to future generations.

ACKNOWLEDGMENTS

I would like to thank my good friends, Bonnie and Joshua Butler, for their companionship over miles of trail, for graciously letting me use their living room floor during the course of my research for this book, and for the use of some of the photos included in it. To my friends Terry Gimbel and Rick Gardner at the Colorado State Forest State Park, thanks for providing me with history, safety, and wildlife insights along the way. Vern Bentley, Hal Wentz, Kathy Kennedy, and Anne Carlstrom at the Routt National Forest also generously shared their knowledge about the Zirkel and Never Summer Wildernesses. Thanks to Dan Hillhouse and my father, Jay Edwards, for the fly fishing scoop. Thanks also to Jim Dustin, editor of the Jackson County Star, for the opportunity to get the word out that North Park is where it's at.

I thank the staff members at the Larimer and Jackson County libraries and the North Park Pioneer and Fort Collins museums for their patience and thorough knowledge of local history. Muchissima gracias to Aaron Gale and Krista Smith for their trail companionship. Thanks go to my mother, Carol Edwards, for the Lake Katherine photograph, the help in editing, not to mention her enduring belief in me, throughout the making of this book. And thanks to my husband's parents, Rich and Jeanne Koschnitzki, for passing on a treasure trove of Geological Survey maps, a true heirloom, and for bringing your son into this world to share mother nature with me for a lifetime.

Special thanks go to Chris Mueller at the Jackson County Geological Information Services for his mapmaking expertise and infinite patience with my maniacal perfectionism. Finally, I am immensely grateful to my husband, Ken Koschnitzki, who helped greatly in the editing process and who clocked many a mile and shared many a breathtaking moment with me from the top of a mountain. I couldn't have done it without you, Ken.

I want to acknowledge the contributors who donated funds to cover the cost of producing the maps. Thanks go to North Park State Bank; Flies Only Tackle Shop; Owl Mountain Partnership; Western Environment and Ecology, Inc.; the North Park Chamber of Commerce; the Routt National Forest; Colorado State Forest State Park; North Park KOA; and North Park Odd Fellows Lodge No.
118, I.O.O.F.

I used maps from many sources, including park brochures, flyers, leaflets, city bike-route maps, and county natural-area handouts. However, most of my map information was provided by the U.S. Geological Survey topographical maps and by maps for Routt, Arapaho, and Roosevelt National Forests. I used a wealth of fascinating historical research in an effort to give each hiking trail a richer sense of place. Please see the references section for more information on historical sources.

INTRODUCTION

A SHORT HISTORY OF NORTHERN COLORADO

Geology

The region we now consider northern Colorado once formed the bottom of an ancient seafloor. Only after the sea receded did the Rocky Mountains begin to rear up, turning whole ridges of stone on end along ragged fault lines to form such familiar local sites as the Nokhu Crags near **Cameron Pass,** later spewing volcanic debris over the surface of the new mountain ranges to create the pink-tinged summits of such peaks as Iron Mountain and most of the peaks of the Never Summer Range. Where the Rocky Mountains end and the Great Plains begin stretch the remnants of the ancient seafloor in the form of the Front Range hogbacks.

Soon, the glaciers of the ice ages inched forth, further sculpting the geology beneath the frozen crust, forming clusters of glacial basins where lakes now dot the landscape, natural reservoirs of freshly melted snow. With the ice ages came woolly mammoths, giant beavers and giant camels, and other beasts, followed by hunters, all heading south to escape the increasing ice. These were the Folsom people, and one of the earliest and most important Folsom archaeological sites, Lindenmeir, was discovered in north-central Colorado near the Wyoming border. Other sites, such as a kill site near Livermore, where early peoples chased game over cliffs for thousands of years, conclusively show that people have been living in the area for anywhere from fifteen thousand to forty thousand years (experts disagree upon exact dates).

Ancient Peoples

The Fremont people and their descendants, the Utes, lived in the area now known as Colorado for much of that period. Related to Hopi Pueblo peoples and the Aztecs before them, the Fremont people lived in pit houses; cultivated corn, beans, and squash; and were artisans of beautiful baskets, pottery, and some of the finest petroglyphs. Following one of the long dry periods common to this area, the Fremont people "disappeared." In fact, they didn't disappear at all but merely altered their lifestyle, adopting many of the plains tribes' hunting tactics as the buffalo herds moved in. The descendants of the Fremont people spoke a Shoshonian language (the Utes and Shoshone are interrelated tribes).

The Utes were no longer agrarian but instead a nomadic people who traveled from the mountains to the edge of the plains by way of the Ute Trail that cuts through much of northern Colorado and traverses many passes that to this day are still called Ute Pass. (North Park has two Ute passes, one over the Park Range, another over the Medicine Bow Range. They are almost directly across the valley from each other.) The Ute Trail was actually three trails: the Big Trail from the Flat Top Mountains, the Dog Trail through the Fall River drainage, and the Child's Trail by way of Windy Gulch. The many bands of Utes lived throughout the mountains of Colorado, hunting buffalo only "as far out into the plains as the shadows of the Rockies stretch at sunset." Their name for themselves means "People of the Shining Mountains," and their creation stories reflect their love of the Colorado mountains.

The Cache la Poudre River is commonly known to have been the dividing line between cultures. Beyond it lived the plains tribes—the Arapaho, the Cheyenne, the Pawnee, and the Sioux. The two cultural groups often clashed over their favorite hunting grounds. The plains tribes had moved down from the north and east, abandoning their former agrarian ways for a hunting lifestyle and following the scattered herds of buffalo, antelope, elk, and deer.

Trappers, Miners, and Homesteaders

In the early 1800s, trappers in search of beaver pelts began trickling into the region, following the edge of the Rockies as the easiest route west. Many of them used the North Fork of the Poudre River through what we now know as the **Red Feather Lakes** area to make their passage in search of better routes into the mountains.

Although North Park has changed little since those days, the trappers came in search of it first, prizing it as the headwaters of the North Platte, a place long beloved by the Utes and Shoshone for its hunting grounds. North Park was the last of the large Colorado parks to be explored, and the first trappers called it New Park to distinguish it from Old Park and Middle Park. Other explorers knew it by its Arapaho name, *de-cay-a-que*, or "the buffalo bullpen," a reference to the walled, circular shape of North Park that provided the big game with the best summer grazing.

North Park is some forty miles long and thirty miles wide, ringed by the Medicine Bow Range to the east, the Park Range to the west, the Rabbit Ears and Never Summer ranges to the south, and the North Platte cutting a course through the mountains to the north. The mountain snows drain into the valley floor by way of an infinite number of creeks, large and small, all of them flowing in a giant web across the valley and inevitably into the North Platte River. With all the water in North Park, it is interesting that no species of trout were native to these waters. Originally, suckers and chubs had the place to themselves. But the beaver populations thrived, along with many other species of game, and the wave of trappers continued.

In 1827, Tom Smith and his party numbered among the first white explorers to visit North Park. In a battle with Indians, Smith was shot through the leg by an arrow. After failing to convince one of his group to help him, he was forced to cut off his own leg and afterward went by the name "Peg Leg."

In 1839, Jim Baker, Bill Williams, and William Sublette also trapped in North Park. Kit Carson came in 1841, reporting back to John C. Fremont, who made his exploratory journey to North Park in 1844 in search of the origins of the North Platte. About his entry through **Northgate Canyon,** Fremont noted that "the valley narrowed as we ascended, and presently degenerated into a gorge, through which the river passed as through a gate. We entered it, and found ourselves in the New Park—a beautiful circular valley of thirty miles diameter, walled in all round with snowy mountains, rich with water and with grass, fringed with pine on the mountainsides below the snow line, and a paradise to all grazing animals."

By 1879, silver was discovered in the south end of North Park, and the community of **Teller City** was established. It was a boomtown, with nearly 1,300 people moving in to build small cabins, a hotel, a newspaper office, a blacksmithing business, and some twenty-seven saloons. A second boomtown, **Lulu City,** located just over the mountains, rode the wave of the mining craze too. In 1882, a toll road was built over

Cameron Pass. There was even a gold rush in Larimer County to the town of Manhattan in the Red Feather Lakes area. But by 1883, it was clear that the expense of shipping and processing the ore was more of a stumbling block than merely getting it out of the ground. People deserted Teller City so fast their belongings were found left where they fell, clothes still hanging in the closets. (Some of these historic objects can be viewed at the Pioneer Museum in Walden. See the "Services Listing" at the back of the book.) Lulu City and Manhattan also met the same end, and today little more than a few old scattered log foundations can be found in their locations.

In the Teller City days, North Park was part of Grand County. But not long after the town's demise, North Park became part of Larimer County as more and more people moved into the fertile valley homesteaded by Antoine Janis.

Janis came as a young boy with his father trapping beaver, just as did many other French-Americans of the time. It was Antoine Janis who verified the reason for the name "Cache la Poudre River," swearing he'd been there the day his father and some other trappers had stashed their gunpowder near the modern-day town of Bellvue to lighten the load of their wagon. Soon he began working as a Sioux trader out of Fort Laramie. He married a relative of Red Cloud, First Elk Woman, and by 1859 had settled down to raise their twelve children. Unlike many trappers of the time who had second wives back East, he was faithful to his Sioux wife and lived out his long life with her. He considered his chosen town site "the loveliest spot on earth," and many other French trappers and their Indians wives apparently agreed. They named their town Corona but later changed it to Laporte, a reminder of its place as a "gateway" from the plains to the mountains. A fort was established nearby and became known as Fort Collins. The fort never required stockades or many reinforcements, however, because for many years, the settlers of the area enjoyed good relations with the Arapaho tribe that lived in the vicinity, thanks to Chief Friday.

Chief Friday was orphaned at a young age when a raiding tribe attacked his village. Stumbling upon the battle scene, the famous trapper Thomas Fitzpatrick discovered and adopted the child, naming him Friday for the day he'd been found. Fitzpatrick sent the young Arapaho to a school in St. Louis, where he adapted well and learned to speak English fluently. In 1838, while hunting, Fitzpatrick and Friday happened across an Arapaho village where his mother recognized him and welcomed him to return to the Arapaho way of life. He did so, but even after many years, Chief Friday always remained friends with Fitzpatrick.

Later in life, Chief Friday was chosen to lead a small band of Arapahos who lived along the Cache la Poudre River. As racial tensions mounted and all Indians were required to move onto reservations, Chief Friday argued for the establishment of a reservation along the Poudre River near Box Elder Creek on the plains, but the Cherokee Trail stage route ran through the area, and several white families were already homesteading it. Fighting between whites and Indians had broken out all over the West following the massacre at Sand Creek, and Chief Friday's clan began to desert him when he refused to preach anything other than compromise with the whites. He led the remains of his small band to join the Shoshones on the Wind River Reservation in Wyoming, but a group of angry whites had tracked them from Fort Collins and attacked, killing four of his clan.

Chief Friday lived out his days in Wyoming, far from his beloved Poudre River, dying of heart disease in 1881.

A Dark Era

In 1878, once the town of Fort Collins had begun to prosper, the mixed Indian families of Laporte were given an ultimatum: Either send their Indian wives to the new reservation in Pine Ridge, South Dakota, or join them there. Antoine Janis chose to leave with First Elk Woman. He died on the Pine Ridge Reservation in 1890, just before the massacre at Wounded Knee.

The tension was growing between the white settlers flooding the Front Range of Colorado and the Indian tribes who still considered the area their home. In 1849, having been forced from their homelands in Georgia, the Cherokee chose to head to California on the rush for gold— they had learned the gold mining trade that had led to the confiscation of their lands. Along the way, they discovered the yellow rock along Cherry Creek that caused a surge of settlers to descend on the area that is now Denver. The Cherokee Trail proved to be the best way west, and the Overland Trail stagecoach line followed the route that is now roughly Highway 287 to Laramie, Wyoming, carrying more and more settlers into what is now northern Colorado.

On November 29, 1864, John M. Chivington's third regiment descended on a camp of peaceful Arapaho and Cheyenne along Sand Creek. Although Sand Creek lies far to the east on the Kansas border, the siege had widespread effects on Colorado history and changed the course of American Indian relations in the United States forever. The massacre left 105 women and children and 28 men dead, only 9 of them warriors. Only a few months before, Black Kettle, chief of the Southern Cheyennes, had staged a peaceful surrender, leading 2,000 people out of the wilderness to speak with Governor John Evans in Denver, who agreed to see them only because they had traveled 400 miles to do so. Evans did not want peace. He said, "But what shall I do with the third regiment?

They have been raised to kill Indians, and they must kill Indians." After being installed on the Sand Creek Reservation, the tribes found their rations had been cut; they had been left to starve. Because Chivington did not want to attack the Indians while they were still on reservation land, he had released them to hunt buffalo just days before the massacre. With most of the warriors out on the hunt, very few were in camp to defend the women, children, and elderly from the brutality of the third regiment.

The survivors of Sand Creek fled in every direction, some of them joining forces with Red Cloud's Sioux to the north, recounting tales of white treachery and brutality that fed the fear and mistrust of the Indian tribes far and wide. Other survivors began staging massive retaliations, cutting telegraph lines and attacking stage stations up and down the Cherokee Trail. Martial law was declared for the state of Colorado, and all adult men were required to join forces against the Indians. One of the strongholds was near the Cache la Poudre River near Fort Collins, and many area homesteaders participated in the ensuing battles.

Only fifteen years later, the Meeker massacre sealed the fate of Native Americans in Colorado. After a treaty signed by Chief Ouray in 1863 designated all the land west of the Continental Divide to the Utes, their lands were whittled down to 16 million acres on the Western Slope. Nathan C. Meeker was a poet and agrarian utopian assigned to the job of Indian agent of the White River Reservation. Although the reservation had plenty of wild game to be hunted, and the Utes there could have continued living much as they had for hundreds of years, Meeker insisted they learn how to grow the corn, beans, and squash that their people had taught the whites to grow not so long before. In his writings, Meeker implied that reservation land belonged to the government and the Indians were mere tenants on it. His words fueled a campaign by Governor Fredrick W. Pitkin and an editor/politician, William Vickers, to rid the state of the last of its Indians.

The campaign was launched under the banner "The Utes Must Go!" One tactic was to blame the Utes for many forest fires (that occurred during a year of drought), one of them on Arapaho Ridge in North Park. As a final stroke, Meeker attempted to plow a field where the tribe grazed horses and ran footraces, insisting that perhaps the Utes had too many horses and that some of them ought to be killed. The plowman was shot, and violence broke out on the reservation. In the end, Meeker was killed, and his wife and daughter were kidnapped. After receiving a message requesting protection, the cavalry dispatched 250 soldiers to White River. After much fighting, the bands of Utes fled in every direction. One group spent the winter near the North Sand Hills in North Park, and the lodge could still be seen a hundred years later. Governor Pitkin's response to the massacre was grim: "My idea is that, unless removed by the government, [the Utes] must necessarily be exterminated." It was a dark era on the Western frontier. After some negotiation, the Utes were assigned to three small reservations, two in the southernmost part of Colorado and a third larger one in Utah.

Into the Present

The cities along the Front Range continued to flourish, including the town of Fort Collins. The Zimmerman family's grand Keystone Hotel, near where the Home Moraine RV park now sits in the upper end of the Poudre Canyon, prospered, especially after a road passable to cars was built through the canyon by a crew of convicts in the early 1900s. Although the grand old hotel was torn down when the U.S. Fish and Game installed stocking ponds, many Poudre Canyon place-names are attributable to the Zimmerman family, including **Zimmerman Lake** and **Lake Agnes**.

In 1914, a mountaineering club headed by Harriet Vaille from the Estes Park area decided it was time to bring order to the names of the mountains, lakes, and passes of the high country, and a naming party was organized. It included three Arapaho tribal members who provided the place-names of northern Colorado's mountain country as they knew and remembered them. The three were Gun Griswold, 73, an elder of the tribe who brought only an eagle-feather fan on the long, grueling journey; Sherman Sage, 63, chief of police of the Northern Arapaho; and Tom Crispin, 38, their interpreter. Also in the party were Shep Husted, an Estes Park guide who conducted the two-week trip, and two friends of his. Many place-names discussed in this book were set down by the naming party of 1914.

Jackson County has since become its own governing body separate from Larimer County, and its boundaries roughly follow the tops of the ridge of mountains that encircle North Park. The silver miners of Teller City had turned to ranching to survive and moved into the center of the valley where the grasses were the highest and the rivers flowed the deepest. The county seat initially had many names—Point of the Rocks, Godfrey, Sage Hen Springs, and Sagebrush among them—but finally everyone settled on the name Walden after the homesteader who settled the spot near the confluence of the Michigan and Illinois Rivers. Logging, mining, and ranching enabled the area to remain self-sufficient for many years. Currently, tourism to the area continues to pick up as visitors learn of the area's wildlife, fly fishing, and old-fashioned feel. In the late 1970s, moose were released into the riparian habitats of North Park and have flourished there, much as they did in the past. Estimates are that North Park boasts some 600 to 700 moose, and their numbers continue to migrate into outlying areas. Hence, visitors will see signs posted claiming that North Park is "the moose-viewing capital of Colorado."

It is the Cache la Poudre River carving its way through the sheer rock of the Poudre Canyon that has always connected the mountains and the plains; the river is like an arbitrary mark scratched in the dust separating ancient cultures and providing a gateway from one world to another. On October 2, 1968, Congress approved the Wild and Scenic River Act, and in 1973, the Poudre River became one of sixty-seven rivers in the United States to be included, and the only one in Colorado. At a dedication ceremony designating thirty-one miles of the river as wild, the Poudre River's water was mixed with samples from eight other wild rivers. Two Cheyenne tribal members blessed the water, and a portion was returned to the river, a symbolic gesture that expressed the importance of wild places to all communities that know and love them.

Northern Colorado's history continues to be made, as populations of people move into the West and the art of living skillfully in proximity to nature is made possible. This art means never forgetting the lessons of the past or the goal of preserving wilderness—its diversity, its challenges, its infinite mystery—for future generations.

HOW TO USE THIS BOOK

Organization

This book is organized by regions and alphabetically within those regions to make finding the right hiking destination easier.

Ratings

Rating a trail as strenuous, moderate, or easy is an art, primarily a subjective one, and cannot be based solely on elevation gains. I do a lot of hiking and consider myself in pretty good shape. Although I have attempted to rate each hike fairly, my idea of what is strenuous may or may not be the same as the next person's. For a more detailed analysis of the difficulty of each trail, check the elevation gains and read the trail descriptions for a better idea of terrain and trail conditions.

Maps

The maps in this book are not intended to replace detailed topographical quadrant maps or to give detailed road plans. They should be used to get you to the trailhead and to help you plan your trip. Each trail description identifies the U.S.G.S. (U.S. Geological Survey) maps that coordinate with the area; in the cases of long, remote trips, I recommend bringing along a topographical map of some sort. Forest Service maps are good backcountry road maps. Forest Service trail numbers are included here to help locate them on Forest Service maps. State and county park trails are not numbered.

Mileage

Trail mileages have been taken with a pedometer and rounded to the nearest quarter mile to eliminate the problems of trying to pinpoint the ever-elusive precise distance. Many mileages were taken more than once and compared with digital counts and Forest Service or park mileages, when possible. Road mileages were done the same way. To compensate for the inexact science of measuring mileage, I have provided detailed descriptions of landmarks and mileposts when possible, letting you know what to watch out for and when you've gone too far.

Bold Type

The use of **boldface type** for a trail name indicates that the trail can be found among the hiking spots described in this book.

Abbreviations

Following are some abbreviations that appear in this guide:

- CR   County Road
- FR   Forest Road
- 4WD   Four-wheel-drive
- SH   State Highway
- U.S.G.S.   U.S. Geological Survey

Mountain Biking

This guide does not cover mountain biking in any thorough fashion. Where mountain biking is allowed on a hiking trail, I have made an effort to indicate that. Mountain biking is not allowed in wilderness areas such as the Cache la Poudre Wilderness, Zirkel Wilderness, or Rawah Wilderness or in Rocky Mountain National Park.

Elevations

I obtained elevations using topographical maps with the intent not of estimating exact altitudes but rather only of giving the book user an idea of elevation gain. Exceptions to this were in establishing summit high points that are based on the most current U.S.G.S. topographical measurements. Also, on loop trails, the ending-elevation estimate is for the spot where the trail begins its return trip.

Backcountry Ethics

The "Leave No Trace" style of backpacking is not a matter of following a set of rules and regulations set down by the Forest Service or anyone else. To those who practice it religiously, it is a way of life. Here are a few guidelines.

Fires and Camp Stoves

- Use a camp stove instead of starting an open fire.
- If you do make a campfire, use a fire ring that has been left behind by previous campers.
- Campfires must be 100 feet, or 40 adult paces, from any source of water.
- If no fire ring can be found, disassemble the one you build when you go, leaving no trace of coals or burnt stones.
- Before leaving, make sure all coals are cool to the touch.

Water

- Always choose a campsite at least 100 feet, or 40 adult paces, from any water source.
- Never use soap to wash hands or dishes directly in the water; instead, carry water at least 50 feet from the water's edge and wash there.
- Cattle do graze on most forest land, including wilderness areas, and giardia and other waterborne critters can be suspended in what appears to be pure mountain water. Bring along a purification pump or tablets. Always consider whether grazing is likely to occur upstream from any water source you use.

Sanitation

- If you pack it in, pack it out. That means everything. Peanut shells, toilet paper, and aluminum foil too. Orange peels, in the dry climate of Colorado, can take years to decompose.

- Always dig a cat hole for human waste. A small spade comes in handy for digging the 8- to 10-inch hole. It's best to carry out the t.p.

- ...Go the extra step and carry out any trash you might find left behind by previous campers.

Livestock

- Use low-impact stock-control techniques such as hobbles, high-lines, pickets, and the like.

- Move your stock frequently to prevent overgrazing.

- Spread manure piles before leaving.

- Call the state or national forest you intend to visit to find out specific regulations concerning certified hay. As of this writing, the Zirkel Wilderness does not allow any hay, not even certified, to stop the spread of noxious weeds; the Rawah Wilderness does allow certified hay.

Other Considerations

- Stay on the trail as it appears it was intended to go whenever possible, even if it means getting boots muddy. They'll dry. In the high country, erosion can take decades to heal itself.

- When crossing alpine tundra, where trails often grow over, try to walk on rocks or snow.

- Instead of picking wildflowers, take a picture or bring along a wildflower guide and identify them.

- Invest in a good pair of binoculars for wildlife viewing. Binoculars will help you to resist the urge to approach wild creatures and will provide you the opportunity to observe them engaged in their natural behavior.

- Travel in small groups and try to maintain quiet voices at all times.

Safety Concerns

Summer Thunderstorms

- Expect afternoon thunderstorms when backpacking or day hiking in northern Colorado's mountains, and plan accordingly.

- If you intend to hike above timberline, get started as early as you can and plan to be back to your car by early afternoon.

- Always bring rain gear and extra layers of clothing.

Dehydration

- Always carry plenty of water. The thin, dry air of the higher altitudes can cause the nausea and headaches of dehydration.

- In the lower elevations, bring extra water when hiking during the hot part of the day. In these areas, 100-degree weather is not uncommon, and many trails at this elevation provide little shade.

- Don't expect to find water along the trail.

- Dehydration is also a concern in the winter season. If you sweat, you're losing moisture that must be replaced.

Hypothermia

- Hypothermia is caused by the drop in body core temperature, causing disorientation, shivers that eventually lead to numbness and imaginary warmth, and, worst of all, bad judgment.

- Winter or summer, carry an extra layer of dry clothing.

- Always carry an emergency blanket, available at any sporting supply store.

Insects

- North Park is notoriously mosquito-ridden in the breeding months of June and July. If you can't endure mosquitoes, plan your trip around these times.

- Mosquitoes like wet, marshy places at any altitude, high or low.

- If you detest wearing chemical insect repellents, as I do, try wearing long pants and sleeves or invest in an inexpensive mosquito-netting hood.

Bears

- Black bears, although rarely seen, can follow their noses into campgrounds and backcountry camps. Never keep anything with a strong odor in your tent with you (including toothpaste and sunscreen), and hang food bags in a tree away from camp.

- Sleep well away from where you cook your meals.

Mountain Lions

- Mountain lions are an even rarer sight than bears. They prefer rocky hillsides and lower elevations.

- Travel in pairs or small groups, and always keep children and pets close by.

Moose

- Expect to encounter moose when hiking in North Park. Moose are not aggressive, but they are defensive, especially of their young or during the fall mating season.

- Moose seem almost tame, in comparison with their deer and elk cousins. Do not approach them, however. If you observe the hackles on the back of their necks rise or see them looking back at you, retreat immediately. They aren't above charging—especially cows with calves and bulls during the autumn mating season.

Rattlesnakes

- Rattlesnakes are common residents of the rocky terrain of the Front Range foothills. Wear high boots and long pants, and never put a hand or foot under a rock ledge where you can't see. North Park and the high country do not have many rattlers.

Dogs on the Trail

- Different people have different opinions on the issue of dogs on our public trails. As you may have noticed by the dedication at the beginning of this book, hiking and dog companionship are intrinsically entwined in my experience. However, I firmly believe that it is the responsibility of dog owners to have complete control over their own dog and to follow forest and park regulations strictly. Fulfilling this responsibility would help to change the bad rap dogs have gotten over the years. It would be a shame to see dogs banned from our public lands altogether. Dogs have every right to join us on the trail and to enjoy the natural world in our company, but the only way to keep that door open is to follow some basic guidelines.

- Do not allow your dog to harass the wildlife.

- Know the leash laws. Whereas Roosevelt National Forest requires leashes, Routt National Forest accepts the control of verbal command. All state and county parks require leashes.

- Clean up after your dog. (Clearing a mess off the trail is a basic common courtesy.)

- Be honest with yourself about how threatening your dog is to other visitors along the trail or how invasive the animal is of their space. If necessary, step aside until others pass. The gesture is usually appreciated.

- Train your dog to respond to basic verbal commands that can be used on the trail.

Emergency Kits and Supplies

- Although this is not a comprehensive list, it may help to get you thinking about what you might need. A good emergency kit should include the following: pocket knife, waterproof fire source, waterproof fire tinder (laundry-dryer lint works well), needle and thread, emergency blanket, map and compass, rain gear, sterile bandages and dressings, topical ointment, ibuprofen or other pain reliever, length of rope or cord, emergency water-purification tablets, snakebite kit, whistle, magnifying glass, sunscreen, and emergency candy (the sugar provides a needed boost of energy in an emergency situation).

- Always carry water and extra clothing layers.

OVERVIEW MAP

This book is laid out in three parts: Fort Collins area, Poudre Canyon area, and North Park area. Using the overview map provided on the following pages, it is possible to find a hike or ski trail you want and to see where it is located in relation to major cities and highways. The numbers on the overview map correspond with the numbers used for each of the trail descriptions listed in the book. This will hopefully make it easier for you to plan a trip to and orient yourself with northern Colorado, which also means getting to the trail faster!

Map Key

Mountain Pass / Building / Other Structure
Summit
Parking Area
Trailhead
Main Trail(s)
Other Trail(s)
US Highway Shield
State Highway Shield
County Road Shield
US Forest Road Shield
Secondary / Forest / 2-Track Road
City / County Road / State Highway
Rivers / Streams
Lakes / Reservoirs
County, Park Boundary

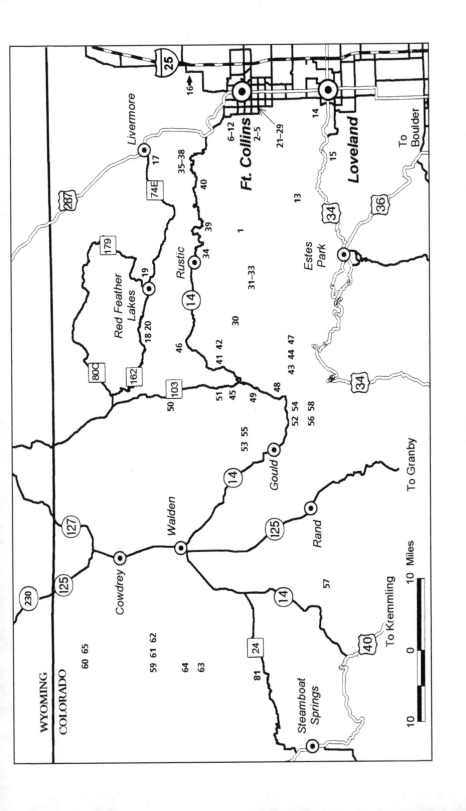

FORT COLLINS AREA TRAILS

BUCKHORN CANYON

Buckhorn Canyon, located just west of Fort Collins, accesses some little-known corners of the Roosevelt National Forest. If solitude is your goal, try exploring the rolling mountains to be found in this locale. Much of the area has not been improved, and you can expect to be traveling some rough 4WD roads. **Lookout Mountain,** listed here, is a good jumping-off trail for longer treks into the remote high country of Rocky Mountain National Park and Pingree Park.

Lookout Mountain Trail #926

▶ **3.5 miles one way**   ▶ **Moderate**

Maps: U.S.G.S. Crystal Mountain
Beginning Elevation: 8,800 feet
Ending Elevation: 10,626 feet
Access Road: Rough 4WD road last 2.5 miles
Season: Midsummer to fall
Connector Trails: Signal Mountain Trail #934

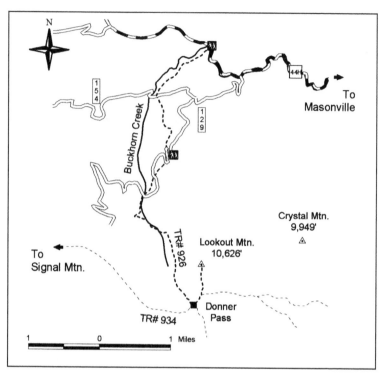

Lookout Mountain Trail #926

Highlights: The arduous drive is rewarded with a great walk through well-mixed forest to a mountaintop for views into Rocky Mountain National Park and the surrounding area.

To Get There

From downtown Fort Collins, take Mulberry Street west to Overland Trail Road, following it north to the Bingham Hill turnoff on the left. Continue to the town of Bellvue. At the stop sign, make a right. At the historic Bellvue Store, turn left onto Rist Canyon Road (CR 54E), continue 17 miles over steep (but paved) mountain roads to Stove Prairie

View of Lookout Mountain's west peak from its east peak with Signal Mountain visible in the background.

Road (CR 27), and turn left. Drive to the 21-mile point where CR 27 meets the junction with Buckhorn Road (CR 44H) and turn right. From here, the road is gravel. Soon after mile marker 30, turn left onto a 4WD track marked Baller Road (FR 129). Baller Road is a high-clearance-only road, a real tire mangler. Take it to the top of a series of switchbacks to the "Trail" sign at the 33.5-mile point. A camping spot and parking are available at the trailhead.

For those without a 4WD, it's also possible to start the trail off Buckhorn Road at a Forest Service facility located after mile marker 32. Add about 2 miles to the hiking mileage.

The Hike

From the parking area, walk across the road past the trailhead display and begin climbing through stands of aspens mixed with lodgepole pines. Soon you will see Lookout Mountain, a pointy-topped landmark to the south with no timberline despite its elevation of 10,626 feet. Panoramas also sweep down into a vast bowl-shaped basin scooped away by ancient glaciers. The trail provides tricky footing, littered with projecting stones and exposed roots. At a trail fork at 0.5 mile, follow the Donner Pass sign to the left. Soon the climb takes you into Douglas firs and, higher yet, into thick, welcoming spruce forests. An old logging pile with gray slabs stacked two stories high serves as a reminder of the area's logging past but with few scars left behind to show for it.

At 2.5 miles, you reach Donner Pass, a crossroads hidden deep in the forest, a saddle with too much tree cover for views. Lookout Mountain Trail is a great jumping-off trail to a multitude of other destinations. A sign at Donner Pass points west 3 miles to Signal Mountain on the boundary of the Comanche Peak Wilderness, while trail #926 continues straight to a trailhead on the North Fork of the Big Thompson River.

To ascend Lookout Mountain, go left (east) at Donner Pass, following signs. A sign 0.25 mile from the pass again points left. Follow the trail another 0.75 mile to a saddle among the limber pines, a tree that prefers the rocky, exposed terrain of this elevation. Watch for Clark's Nutcrackers, a bird that collects and buries huge caches of the seeds of the limber pine cones to get it through the winter.

The saddle appears to be the top of the mountain, making one wonder at the name because the trees are too numerous to look out through. But, hark, you are standing in the bosom of the mountain. Lookout Mountain is double-peaked. From the saddle you can choose to climb either one (or both!) of the rocky caps to the east and west of the saddle for 360-degree vistas into the Mummy Range and Rocky Mountain National Park. Signal and South Signal Mountains are the nearest mountains to the west with Stormy Peaks beyond. Mount Dickinson (11,831 feet) and Mount Dunraven (12,571 feet) lord over the views into the national park to the southwest. Crystal Mountain is the lower mountain to the northeast.

HORSETOOTH MOUNTAIN PARK

If you want to hike to the summit of the most famous landmark in the Fort Collins area, this is the place. **Horsetooth Rock** caps the top of Horsetooth Mountain Park, a large tract of county-managed wilderness that spans one-half the length of the western shore of Horsetooth Reservoir and borders Lory State Park to the north, which spans the other half of the reservoir.

Unlike Lory State Park, which limits mountain biking access, Horsetooth Mountain Park with its never-ending web of a trail system is heaven for mountain bikers, and hikers can expect to share the trail with them. Longer hikes or mountain bike rides can be made by way of two trails connecting the parks. If you are looking for a long, challenging backpacking trip or just a short jaunt, this park provides.

Unfortunately, the county park has seen fit to charge a $6 entrance fee, and even an annual pass is a hefty $60 and provides admittance only to Larimer County parks. If you agree that access to our wilderness areas should be available to all, not just those with enough spare cash, let a county park ranger know. Keep in mind that dogs must be leashed at all times inside the park.

Herrington/Stout Loop

▶ 8.75-mile loop ▶ Moderate

Maps: U.S.G.S. Horsetooth Reservoir

Beginning Elevation: 5,762 feet

Ending Elevation: 6,510 feet

Access Road: Paved county road

Season: Year-round, depending on weather

Connector Trails: Horsetooth Rock Trail and **Spring Creek/Mill Creek Trail,** along with many other overlapping trails.

Highlights: Views! The question is what can't you see on this loop in a little-known corner of Horsetooth Mountain Park.

To Get There

From downtown Fort Collins, take Mulberry Street west to Taft Hill Road and head south to the Harmony Street intersection. Turn right (west) onto CR 38E and take it around the reservoir to the Horsetooth Mountain Park parking area on the left. Be sure to pay the $6 daily pass fee before embarking on your hike.

The Hike

Be sure to carry a map of the area when doing this hike. The trails in the Horsetooth Mountain Park area are well-posted but convoluted, and nowhere more so than on this hike. However, bear with it. It's worth the effort.

From the parking area, locate the foot trail that takes off just to the right of the service road. After a short jaunt through the mahogany brush

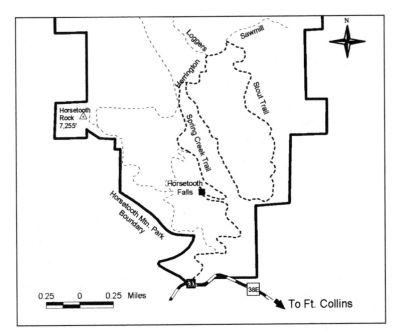

Herrington/Stout Loop

hillsides, you'll find the path meets a fork. Go right, following signs to **Horsetooth Falls.** At 1.75 miles, you will see the side trail off to the falls. Notice the canyon wall above the falls to the east. The Stout Loop Trail takes you along the ridge up there to mingle with the eagles.

At 1.25 miles, the trail meets a three-way junction: To the left is the Soderberg Trail to **Horsetooth Rock,** and uphill to the right is the beginning of the **Spring Creek Trail.** Continue up the hill, following the Spring Creek Trail for a short distance to yet another trail junction with the Wathen Trail, a backdoor route to Horsetooth Rock. Stay with the Spring Creek Trail as it winds up the long meadowy draw giving good views of Horsetooth Rock.

At the Herrington Trail junction, go right, heading east uphill into the ponderosa pine forest. At an overlook with views of the reservoir, the trail meets a T. The Larimer County Parks map, distributed at the trailhead, is of little help in orienting yourself at this point. Picturing Herrington and Stout as one trail helped me make sense of it. The description here is provided in a counterclockwise direction, as if you are heading right on the Stout Trail from the overlook junction, but whichever direction you take, you'll find lots of up and down. Very soon, the trail breaks onto open hillsides, giving you views of Long's Peak over one shoulder, and the reservoir, city, and plains over the other as the trail descends the long ridge. Horsetooth Falls is somewhere w-a-a-a-y down below.

If you're traveling in the heat of summer, bring extra water for the Stout Trail's 3 miles across open hillside with little shade. Much of this section looks down onto the housing developments around Inlet Bay and Dixon Cove, revealing tiny boats coming and going. But soon the trail curves back on its return trip, accessing a drainage choked with ponderosa pine to make the climb back up.

Here, things get somewhat messy, with several small trails being used to complete the loop. Try to keep yourself as oriented as possible and you'll be fine. At the Stout/Sawmill Trails junction, make a left, heading west up the Sawmill Trail. At the junction of Sawmill and Loggers Trails soon after, again go left. At the Loggers/Herrington Trails junction, the Loggers Trail makes a jog to the left to dead-end nearby. Head uphill on Herrington to the right, completing the loop when you reemerge at the Stout/Herrington junction. To make the return trip, simply retrace your steps back to Spring Creek Trail and the parking area.

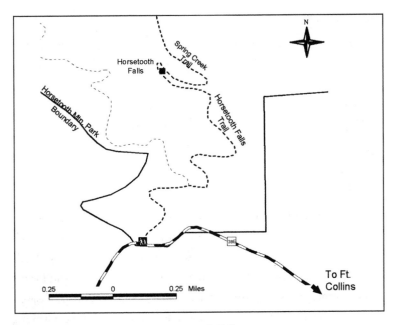

Horsetooth Falls

Horsetooth Falls

▶ **0.75 mile one way**   ▶ **Moderate**

Maps: U.S.G.S. Horsetooth Reservoir

Beginning Elevation: 5,762 feet

Ending Elevation: 5,800 feet

Access Road: Paved road

Season: Year-round, depending on weather

Connector Trails: Soderberg Trail, **Spring Creek Trail**

Highlights: A short walk through the wildflower hillsides to a cascade over a high precipice. A local favorite.

To Get There

From downtown Fort Collins, take Mulberry Street west to Taft Hill Road and head south to Harmony Street. At the Taft Hill/Harmony intersection, turn right (west) onto CR 38E and continue around Horsetooth Reservoir a few miles to the Horsetooth Mountain Park parking lot on the left. Road signs indicate the way. Be sure to pay the $6 daily pass fee before starting your hike.

The Hike

From the parking area, locate the foot path taking off just past the service road entrance behind the farthest picnic area. Walk up through mahogany-brush hillsides to the Horsetooth Falls/Soderberg Trails junction. Go right here, dropping down over the ridge. The wildflowers grow in profusion spring through late summer on these open hillsides, one variety giving way to another as the sun's rays bend. A bench along the path provides a good spot to take a breather or just to sit and enjoy the views of Spring Creek Canyon carving its way down to cut a gash in the hogbacks. Flooded, this gap is now known as Inlet Bay of Horsetooth Reservoir. Views along the path are also good of the high canyon wall above Spring Creek. A trail loop known as the **Herrington/Stout Loop** takes the ambitious trekker along the very lip of this canyon wall.

As you continue down toward the bottom of the gorge, the trail crosses a footbridge at a U-shaped rock hollow where a spring supplies moisture for a thicket of deciduous trees and shrubs. This is a fun spot to explore before continuing on to Horsetooth Falls.

Watch for a trail sign pointing out a side trail to the left directing you to the falls. The trail leads back a short distance to yet another hollow encircled by pink granite cliffs and complete with green pools of water in the cool shadows of stone. Because this is the American West and most of our water comes and goes with the passing whims of the weather, there is no guarantee you will find the falls roaring. However, they are

On Spring Creek Trail above Horsetooth Falls

supplemented by the trickle of the permanent spring after which Spring Creek is named, and you can count on at least a nice trickle sprinkling over the soaring cliffs above, creating a lulling sound that attracts birds and wildlife of all sorts during much of the year. If you are determined to see the falls surging with white water, time your trip during spring runoff after a good snowy winter.

Not to be missed is a look at the falls from the top down. Return to the main trail and continue up a series of steep switchbacks along the Spring Creek Trail to an overlook. You can add mileage to your walk by following the **Spring Creek Trail** to the Soderberg junction, where a bench sits next to the pooling springs under the aromatic shade of the ponderosas. A very quiet and meditative spot, a favorite of mine.

Horsetooth Rock

▶ **3.5 miles one way**   ▶ **Moderate**

Maps: U.S.G.S. Horsetooth Reservoir

Beginning Elevation: 5,762 feet

Ending Elevation: 7,255 feet

Access Road: Paved road

Season: Year-round, depending on weather

Connector Trails: Horsetooth Falls Trail, Soderberg Trail, **Spring Creek Trail,** Wathen Trail

Highlights: The hike to the summit of this local landmark takes you past a waterfall and through some fascinating pink rock-strewn terrain for beautiful views.

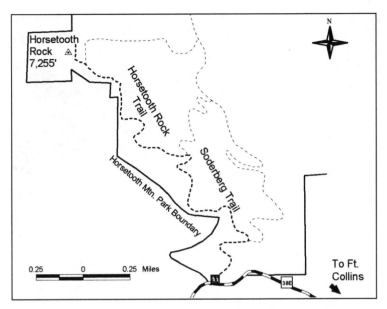

Horsetooth Rock

To Get There

From downtown Fort Collins, take Mulberry Street west to Taft Hill Road and head south to Harmony Street. At the Taft Hill/Harmony intersection, turn right (west) onto CR 38E and continue around Horsetooth Reservoir a few miles to the Horsetooth Mountain Park parking lot on the left. Be sure to pay the $6 daily pass fee before embarking on your hike.

The Hike

From the parking area, locate the foot path taking off just past the service road entrance behind the farthest picnic area. Walk up through mahogany-brush hillsides to the **Horsetooth Falls**/Soderberg Trails fork. Either trail will get you to the top of the mountain, but the

Along the trail to Horsetooth Rock

Soderberg Trail is the more direct. Follow it up at a strenuous climb to the service road intersection. Follow the service road to the 1.5-mile point where you come to the Horsetooth Rock Trail after a short walk up the road. (This service road is a mountain biker's favorite.) Views of the hogbacks and the rocky canyon walls of Spring Creek are good from the trail junction, but Horsetooth Rock itself is not visible until you are directly upon it. The Horsetooth Rock Trail soon contracts to a narrow path winding through the robust ponderosas with close-up views of the granite outcroppings. The rocks provide terracing for a splendid variety of wildflowers, including black-eyed susans, wild geranium, groundsel, and thistle. Soon the trail reencounters the service road, but continue straight on the narrow foot path. As the trail climbs toward the summit, it traverses solid slabs of pink granite. To keep track of the trail, watch for rock cairns.

The first views of the famous landmark are near at hand, and the scene ahead reveals Horsetooth's rosy-hued precipices—an amazing sight at sunrise. Two different stories explain Horsetooth's red tint. The first says that an upswelling of magma, having cooled to produce the igneous granite rock that we see in the area today, pushed up during the tumultuous making of the Rocky Mountains, and it is the flecks of feldspar that stain it. An Arapaho story claims that during a ferocious battle in the sky, the Black Warrior slew the Red Warrior, spilling his blood all over the land. Horsetooth Rock is the remains of the Red Warrior's heart. Hm. Are the stories of upheaval and battling forces really so different?

It is possible to ascend the rock itself by crossing below the landmark to its north side, following rock cairns. The trip up requires a bit of rock-climbing skill but no fancy equipment. Views of the Bellvue Valley open out below you as you pass through a gap in the rocks. The best access point begins beyond this gap. The ascent is not for the weak of stomach, but it is an exhilarating climb that offers a bird's-eye view of the city and plains to the east. Speaking of birds—keep a sharp eye for raptors that nest in the high rock niches.

A good loop back is to take the Wathen Trail (the junction is near the foot of the rock and marked with a sign) down to the **Spring Creek Trail** and return by way of the **Horsetooth Falls Trail.**

Spring Creek/Mill Creek Trail

▶ 6.25 miles one way ▶ Moderate

Maps: U.S.G.S. Horsetooth Reservoir

Beginning Elevation: 5,762 feet

Ending Elevation: 5,800 feet

Access Road: Paved county road

Season: Year-round, depending on weather

Connector Trails: Horsetooth Falls Trail, Soderberg Trail, **Herrington Trail,** Loggers Trail, Lory State Park access.

Highlights: For those with a taste for something longer and more challenging but within easy access from the city, this is your hike. Wildflower meadows, views, and relatively good opportunities for solitude.

To Get There

From downtown Fort Collins, take Mulberry Street west to Taft Hill Road and head south to Harmony Street. At this intersection turn right (west) onto CR 38E and take it around Horsetooth Reservoir to the Horsetooth Mountain Park parking lot on the left. Be sure to pay the $6 daily pass fee before starting your hike.

The Hike

Making a two-car shuttle of this hike would be easy: Simply leave a second vehicle at Lory State Park, eliminating a return trip. (See **Arthur's Rock** for directions.)

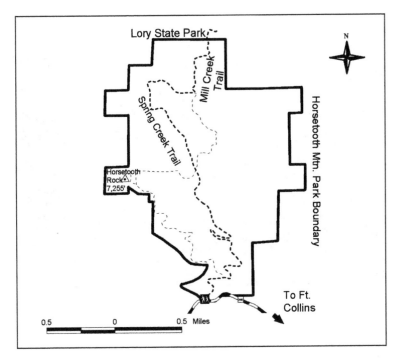

Spring Creek/Mill Creek Trail

From the parking area, locate the foot trail that takes off just to the right of the service road behind a picnic area. After a short stretch through the open hillsides, the path meets a fork. Go right, following signs to **Horsetooth Falls.** At 0.75 mile, you will see the side trail veering off to the falls. It's worth a stop and look, especially during spring runoff.

At 1.25 miles, the trail meets a three-way junction: To the left is the Soderberg Trail to **Horsetooth Rock,** and uphill to the right is the beginning of the Spring Creek Trail. This is a nice spot to sit and enjoy the clean air next to the perennial spring pools and to hear the mourning doves that collect there in the early morning hours.

From here, continue up the hill, following the Spring Creek Trail to yet another junction with the Wathen Trail, a backdoor route to

View from the Spring Creek Trail

Horsetooth Rock. Stay with the Spring Creek Trail as it starts up the long meadowy draw, and take in the good views of Horsetooth Rock to the west. You will also pass the **Herrington Trail** at 2.75 miles on your way up the draw.

The upper corridor of Spring Creek is a beautiful, enchanted place. In the early summer, the meadows along the creek bloom with lavender wild geranium, loco weed, golden pea, and wild iris. The creek is dry except in wet years. Don't miss taking a breather on the somewhat strenuous ascent toward the ridge dividing Spring and Mill Creeks. The views of the gorge and the hogbacks behind you are panoramic.

The Spring Creek Trail terminates where it encounters a wide service road and the beginning of the Mill Creek Trail, which descends through the breezy ponderosa pines. The Mill Creek Trail does what the Spring Creek Trail does but in reverse—plunging down into creek drainages only to climb steeply out of them. At the 5-mile point, the Mill Creek

Trail intersects the Loggers Trail, a short 2.25-mile side path that leads to some old logging ruins.

After winding up and down steep switchbacks into shady Mill Creek itself and a second draw soon after, the path encounters the orange park boundary gate accessing Lory State Park. From the gate, it's another 1.5 miles to Arthur's Rock. For those interested in a good long backpacking trip, campsites are available along the **Timber Trail** near Arthur's Rock. No open fires are allowed inside the state park.

(For those doing the Mill Creek Trail from the Lory State Park end, be aware that there is no sign from the Arthur's Rock Trail pointing out the Mill Creek connection. A sign at the trail fork identifies it as a bike/horse trail, located on the second meadow above the switchbacks and past the **Overlook Trail** junction.)

LORY STATE PARK

Bordering **Horsetooth Mountain Park** on its southern boundary, this state-managed park spans one-half the length of Horsetooth Reservoir's western shore and boasts some of the wildest and most accessible country to be reached from Fort Collins. Many of the most famous local hikes are located inside the state park, including **Arthur's Rock**. The park features some fascinating sandstone hogbacks, and two trails connect it to Horsetooth Mountain Park. Daily admission is $5, but an annual pass of $50 gets you into any of the forty-four state parks, including the Colorado State Forest State Park just on the other side of Cameron Pass, some of the best cross-country skiing to be had. Dogs must be leashed inside the park boundaries, and campfires are not permitted except in designated fire grills.

Arthur's Rock

▶ **1.75 miles one way**   ▶ **Moderate**

Maps: U.S.G.S. Horsetooth Reservoir

Beginning Elevation: 5,520 feet

Ending Elevation: 6,780 feet

Access Road: Good gravel road, all cars

Season: Year-round, depending on weather; trail can be muddy in the spring

Connector Trails: Timber Trail, Overlook Trail, and the **Spring Creek/Mill Creek Trail** to Horsetooth Mountain Park

Highlights: Locally famous rock formation located in Lory State Park with sunflower meadows, waterfalls, and views of Horsetooth Reservoir and the city.

To Get There

To reach Lory State Park from downtown Fort Collins, take Mulberry Street west to Overland Trail Road and turn north. Drive 2.5 miles along curvy Overland Trail Road to Bingham Hill Road and turn left (west). Continue over the hill to the town of Bellvue where you reach a stop sign. Notice the sign posted to Lory State Park. Turn left at this T and drive until you see yet another park sign. Go right here on CR 25G to its dead end at the park's boundary, turning left onto a gravel road. Be sure to stop at the visitor center and pay your $5 daily fee.

To reach the Arthur's Rock trailhead, continue down the gravel road to its end, where you'll find a parking lot and restrooms. This is also the **South Valley** trailhead.

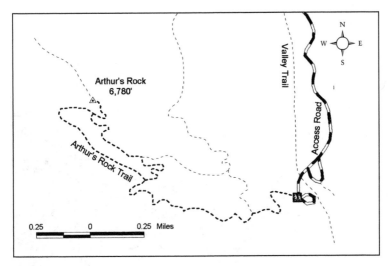

Arthur's Rock

The Hike

The Arthur's Rock Trail begins just to the right of the restrooms and is well posted. It leads up Arthur's Rock Gulch, an enticing slot between looming rock cliffs that usually percolates, complete with small waterfalls, but really roars during periods of runoff. The trail soon ascends to the ridge above the draw and swings around a bend for your first vistas of the Lory sandstone hogbacks and coves that look as if bites have been taken out of them. You then stroll through an open meadow where sunflowers grow tall in late summer. Large cottonwoods grow along the creek. Arthur's Rock, hidden until now, appears above, a proud, south-facing silhouette.

At the meadow, the trail meets up with the **Mill Creek Trail**, accessing Horsetooth Mountain Park. From here begins the more vigorous stretch of trail to the summit. The trail leads into dark north-sloped ponderosa pine forest. Soon the path veers away from the creek bottom, heading straight up the south face of the mountain, a hot and

View from Arthur's Rock

laborious undertaking during summer months. Be sure to bring plenty of water. A second intersection at a lookout point connects with the **Overlook Trail.** From this fork, the path edges around the foot of the massive vertical rock of Arthur's Rock itself, smooth and peach-toned, towering dozens of stories overhead and dazzling at twilight when the rock seems to light up like a lampshade. Continue up through the pine forest, ignoring several hiker-made tracks, then navigate along the trail as it climbs to a small saddle intersecting the **Timber Trail.** Go right here, where you encounter a jumble of large boulders. Hawks and other birds of prey make cliff sides their homes, and almost any visit to Arthur's Rock affords a glimpse of one of the circling hunters. I also spotted a woodpecker hunting insects in one of the many standing dead pines.

It is possible to scramble hand over foot to the summit by skirting the rock along the west side to one of two "cracks" that serve as a staircase or ladder to the flat rock tops, where views of the surrounding area are breathtaking. During one of my visits, I spotted a golden eagle collecting branches for nest building. It's quite a sight to see an eagle soaring below you! Several campsites are available a short distance back along the Timber Trail. No campfires are allowed.

Overlook Trail

▶ **2 miles one way**   ▶ **Moderate**

Maps: U.S.G.S. Horsetooth Reservoir

Beginning Elevation: 5,520 feet

Ending Elevation: 5,480 feet

Access Road: Good gravel road, all vehicles

Season: Year-round, depending on weather

Connector Trails: Arthur's Rock Trail, Mill Creek Trail, and
   Well Gulch Trail

Highlights: This trail is a useful connector trail or a destination in
   itself. Wildflowers and phenomenal views welcome you the entire
   distance.

To Get There

This trail is located inside Lory State Park, a 19.5-mile drive from the suburbs of Fort Collins. To reach the park from downtown Fort Collins, take Mulberry Street west to Overland Trail Road and turn north. Drive along curvy Overland Trail to Bingham Hill Road and turn left, heading west, dropping over the hill into the Bellvue Valley. At the road T, turn left again, following signs to Lory State Park. Just before Horsetooth Reservoir's north dam, turn right onto CR 25G, again following a sign to

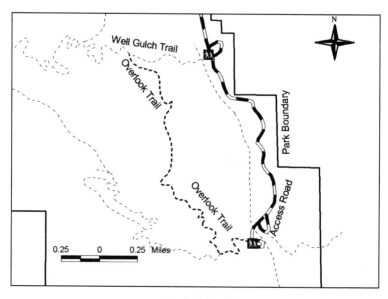

Overlook Trail

the park. Soon you will come to the park's boundary. Follow a gravel road to the visitor center to pay your $5 daily pass fee.

To reach the Overlook Trail, drive to the end of the park's gravel access road and park in the **Arthur's Rock** trailhead parking area. You can hike the trail in the opposite direction from the description given here by parking at the **Well Gulch** trailhead parking area.

The Hike

Although this trail can be done from either direction, I recommend starting from the Arthur's Rock access because it is less strenuous. One section in particular, just past the overlook point, has tricky footing as it slips and slides down a steep incline. It's a difficult battle to come up the other direction.

From the trailhead, walk up the Arthur's Rock Trail, following a creek bed through the narrow keyhole that is the mouth of Arthur's Rock

Along the Overlook Trail

Gulch. The trail immediately switchbacks up onto the ridge above before opening into a large meadow with views of Arthur's Rock where you will spot the well-posted Overlook Trail connection. (The **Mill Creek Trail,** accessing Horsetooth Mountain Park, comes onto the meadow at the other end.) From the meadow, the trail takes you up through boulder fields to a rock outcropping sitting in the deep shadows of Arthur's Rock itself. Here the trail reconnects with the Arthur's Rock Trail a second time. This is the overlook for which the trail is named, and it has good views of the reservoir and the hogbacks, the city and the plains. But the entire stretch of the Overlook Trail provides superb vistas.

After the spot where the descent is tricky, the trail levels off, snaking around below a looming rock overhang to meet Well Gulch. The wildflowers and flowering currant, yucca, and mahogany bushes grow in profusion along this east-facing slope. The views of the reservoir and its blue coves keep the trekker company the entire way. This section of the trail is easy to navigate. I classify it as a moderate trail due to the steep gravely section near the Arthur's Rock Trail junction.

The Overlook Trail ends where it intersects the Well Gulch Trail. An enjoyable loop hike is to walk down Well Gulch toward its trailhead and return to your vehicle by way of the southbound stretch of the Valley Trail.

As a destination trail, the Overlook Trail often goes overlooked itself, providing good opportunities for solitude. However, the trail also is a great loop-maker, especially when you use the **Timber Trail** as an alternative access to Arthur's Rock, returning to the trailhead by way of the Overlook Trail to Well Gulch and back to the parking area via the Valley Trail, a 7.75-mile loop.

Shoreline Trail

▶ **1 mile one way**   ▶ **Moderate**

Maps: U.S.G.S. Horsetooth Reservoir

Beginning Elevation: 5,520 feet

Ending Elevation: 5,540 feet

Access Road: Good gravel road

Season: Year-round, depending on weather

Connector Trails: Valley Trail branch

Highlights: A short jaunt through a gap in the red sandstone hogbacks to a shady cottonwood grove along the shores of Horsetooth Reservoir.

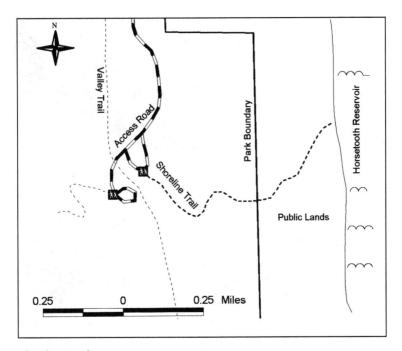

Shoreline Trail

To Get There

To reach Lory State Park from downtown Fort Collins, take Mulberry Street west to Overland Trail Road and turn right (north). Drive 2.5 miles along curvy Overland Trail to Bingham Hill Road and turn left (west). Continue over the hill to the town of Bellvue where you reach a stop sign. Notice the sign posted to Lory State Park. Turn left at this T and drive to CR 25G, where another sign is posted. Turn right here and continue on CR 25G to its dead end at the park's entrance, turning left onto a gravel road. After stopping at the visitor center to pay your $5 daily fee, continue up the access road to the Shoreline Trail parking area on the left, a stone's throw before the **Arthur's Rock** parking area.

Sandstone ridge on the Shoreline Trail

The Hike

The best time to make a trek up into the red sandstone hogbacks of Lory State Park is in the evening when the shimmer of the setting sun seems to glow from inside the cliff walls extending for miles in either direction. This is also a good time to spot deer grazing among the mahogany brush. The Shoreline Trail provides the best trail access up the sandstone ridge for close-up views.

The trail embarks from the back of the parking area behind an information sign and begins meandering up through the mahogany and oak brush hillside, searching out a gap in the ridges of the hogbacks. On this western slope of the ridge, there is very little shade along the trail, and a midday hike in the summertime can be dehydrating. At the 0.5-mile point, after circling around a stunning wall of deep magenta sandstone, the path reaches an intersection; follow it straight, continuing on toward the reservoir soon visible below. The right-hand trail is a branch of the **South Valley Loop** and also worth exploring. Keep in mind that rattlesnakes love the combination of rocks and grasslands found along this trail.

The trail becomes crumbly, skittering down over broken slabs of sandstone, and this feature spells a more strenuous climb on the return trip. Large broad-limbed ponderosas grow along this eastern slope of the hogbacks, providing some measure of shade. Head for the shore below where a mature stand of cottonwoods prospers, a nice place for a cool waterside picnic spot and a doable hiking distance for the whole family. As you return the way you came, take in the magnificent views of Arthur's Rock.

South Valley Loop

▶ 3-mile loop   ▶ Easy

Maps: U.S.G.S. Horsetooth Reservoir

Beginning Elevation: 5,520 feet

Ending Elevation: 5,400 feet

Access Road: Good gravel road, all cars

Season: Year-round, depending on weather

Connector Trails: Horsetooth Mountain Park Trail (Nomad Trail)

Highlights: Views of famous **Arthur's Rock** from a meadow walk to a reservoir cove boasting lovely sandstone formations and wildflowers.

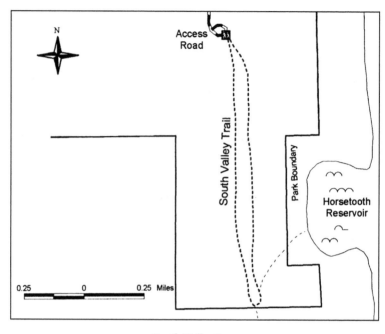

South Valley Loop

To Get There

This trail is located inside Lory State Park, a 19.5-mile drive from the suburbs of Fort Collins. To reach the park from downtown Fort Collins, take Mulberry Street west to Overland Trail Road and turn north. Drive 2.5 miles along curvy Overland Trail to Bingham Hill Road, continuing to the 4.5-mile point where you reach a stop sign in the town of Bellvue. Turn left here, noticing the sign posted to Lory State Park. Turn right just before the northernmost dam of Horsetooth Reservoir onto CR 25G (again a sign is posted). Take CR 25G to the park's boundary, being sure to stop at the visitor center to pay your $5 daily fee.

To reach the South Valley Trail, drive to the end of the road to the **Arthur's Rock** parking area. I recommend walking the section of the trail that descends into the meadow on the south side of the parking

Views of the cove on the South Valley Trail

area. Two trails drop off from the parking area to form an enjoyable loop not identified on the Lory State Park maps.

The Hike

This easy stroll down the valley between the foothills, with its red sandstone ridge on one side and the long gentle flank of Arthur's Rock on the other, is a pleasant walk any season. The path takes you through hip-deep prairie grasses, dropping into one bedrock drainage after another, each one a new opportunity for shade and exploration under the boughs of the mature cottonwoods that grow along them. Velvety-leafed mullein and wild primrose grow sheltered among the grasses. The meadow, scattered with horse jumps, is a favorite for horseback riders, and the Valley Trail is currently the only trail open to mountain bikes and horses. As you walk, you'll notice the cove of your destination to the east but feel you're walking right on past it. However, the trail does indeed circle around, offering a more thorough meander across the valley floor.

At 1.5 miles, the South Valley Trail intersects with the Horsetooth Mountain Park Trail (H.M.P.T. on the post at the junction), or the Nomad Trail. To reach your cove, turn left, heading back north to form a loop. From up here, your descent toward the water will give you great views of the red rock formations that cradle the cove in seclusion. The trail leading down to the cove can be overgrown at certain times of year, but watch closely and you'll spot it. You should reach the shore at 1.5 miles, to find Arthur's Rock looming grandly from this spot. A sandy beach encircled by tall, shady cottonwoods, it is a good place for a waterside picnic.

Although not a perfect choice for solitude (it's also a favorite for motorboats when the reservoir is full), it is nevertheless a worthwhile destination at the end of a unique trail. I suggest trying this walk midweek or, even better, in the autumn when the light glowing off the red rocks is particularly magical. The route is also popular with mountain bikers.

The loop brings you back to the parking area via a parallel but lower meadow path. To extend the walk, take the Valley Trail that continues parallel to the road on both sides the length of the park. The eastern side of this extra-long loop provides superb views of the sandstone cliffs and is worth exploring. Keep in mind that you are sharing this habitat with rattlers.

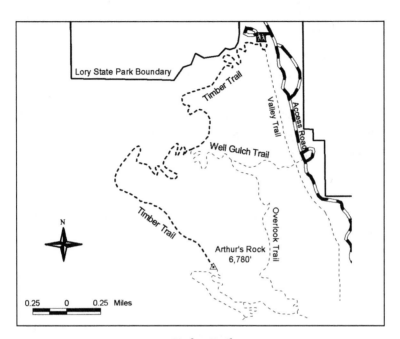

Timber Trail

Timber Trail

▶ 3.5 miles one way ▶ Moderate

Maps: U.S.G.S. Horsetooth Reservoir

Beginning Elevation: 5,520 feet

Ending Elevation: 6,780 feet

Season: Year-round, depending on weather

Connector Trails: Well Gulch, Waterfall Trail, and Arthur's Rock

Highlights: A good backdoor route to Arthur's Rock with views, lush alpine forest, and opportunities for solitude and further exploration.

To Get There

This trail is located inside Lory State Park, a 19.5-mile drive from the suburbs of Fort Collins. To reach the park from downtown Fort Collins, take Mulberry Street west to Overland Trail Road and turn north. Drive 2.5 miles along curvy Overland Trail to Bingham Hill Road and turn left (west), dropping over the hill into the Bellvue Valley. At the road T, turn left, following signs to Lory State Park. Just before Horsetooth Reservoir's north dam, turn right onto CR 25G. Soon you will come to the park's boundary. Be sure to stop at the visitor center to pay your $5 daily pass fee. The Timber/**Waterfall** trailhead is the first one you reach on the right after the visitor center.

The Hike

Before starting on the Timber Trail, take a minute to visit the **Waterfall Trail,** a mere 0.25 mile up a narrow draw accessed behind the restrooms. This spot is beautiful any time of year.

The Timber Trail begins beyond the volleyball pit, climbing through open hillsides of mountain mahogany brush to follow the horseshoe-shaped terrain of Soldier's Canyon as it leads around to meet Well Gulch. This section of trail has a very Mediterranean feel to it with views of the reservoir and its coves all the way.

At the trail junction with Well Gulch, the path embarks on a series of switchbacks up to the top of the ridge where it becomes somewhat strenuous but affords views from above of the cliff-lined gulch below. The trail then plunges into the damp north-facing forest, dense with ponderosa pines and Douglas firs. (You can identify a Douglas fir cone by noticing the spines sticking out of it that resemble the hindquarters of a mouse—little feet and tails!)

At the top, the path meanders through ponderosa pines, accessing several nice campsites. No campfires are allowed in the state park.

Here the forest has a very remote feel and superb potential for further explorations. On my visit, I was fortunate to see a deer lope off into the dark shadowy forest.

Technically, the Timber Trail ends at its intersection with the **Arthur's Rock** trail at 3.5 miles. However, I recommend walking the extra 1 mile farther to access Arthur's Rock.

A good 7.75-mile loop hike is to continue down the Arthur's Rock Trail and use the **Overlook Trail** to Well Gulch as a return route. Just before the Well Gulch trailhead, go north on the Valley Trail to return to your vehicle.

Waterfall Trail

▶ **0.25 mile one way**   ▶ **Easy**

Maps: U.S.G.S. Horsetooth Reservoir

Beginning Elevation: 5,520 feet

Ending Elevation: 5,600 feet

Access Road: Good gravel road, all vehicles

Season: Year-round, depending on weather

Connector Trails: Timber Trail and Valley Trail

Highlights: A short walk into a narrow canyon to a waterfall and fascinating rock sculptures shaped by the perennial flow of water.

To Get There

This trail is located inside Lory State Park, a 19.5-mile drive from the suburbs of Fort Collins. To reach the park from downtown Fort Collins,

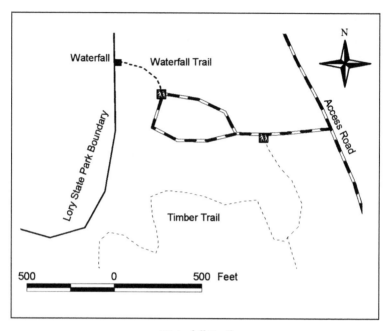

Waterfall Trail

take Mulberry Street west to Overland Trail Road and turn north. Drive 2.5 miles along curvy Overland Trail to Bingham Hill Road and turn left, heading west, dropping over the hill into the Bellvue Valley. At the road T, turn left again, following signs to Lory State Park. Just before Horsetooth Reservoir's north dam, turn right onto CR 25G. Soon you will come to the park's boundary. Follow a gravel road to the visitor center to pay your $5 daily pass fee. The Timber/Waterfall trailhead is the first one you reach on the right after the visitor center.

The Hike

The Waterfall Trail shares a trailhead with the Timber Trail, a 3.5-mile backdoor route to **Arthur's Rock**. From the parking area, the Timber Trail launches off from behind the volleyball pit. A short distance up the Timber Trail, the trail forks. The lower trail is known as the Valley Trail and is currently the only trail in the park open to mountain bikes and horse travel.

To visit the waterfall, walk beyond the restrooms from the picnic area, following signs to your destination. The trail follows a creek bed over a footbridge to the crux of a smoothly carved rock wall where, depending on the time of year, water is either flowing, trickling, or roaring down into the pools below.

The path takes you back into a secret, naturally circular amphitheater a short distance up a narrow, brambly gulch. The best time to visit is during spring runoff or after a good rain. I visited one May after a dry winter and found the waterfall flowing in a gentle trickle that turned the schist rock (the same type that can be found at neighboring **Well Gulch**) a polished black. Be aware that the stones can get slippery when wet, making rock climbing hazardous. The water has rushed over these rocks, sculpting and shaping them, for hundreds of years, to create more of a rock funnel than a waterfall drop. This lush spot is home to a diversity of plant life, and even though roads and buildings are nearby, the place feels isolated and blessed by a special light and a constant seeping of water from the walls of the canyon.

It is possible to rock climb freehand a short distance above the waterfall, but dense brambles choke the canyon and make further investigation difficult.

Well Gulch

▶ **1.5 miles one way**   ▶ **Moderate**

Maps: U.S.G.S. Horsetooth Reservoir

Beginning Elevation: 5,480 feet

Ending Elevation: 6,200 feet

Access Road: Good gravel road, all cars

Season: Year-round, depending on weather

Connector Trails: Timber Trail and the Valley Trail

Highlights: Small canyon near **Arthur's Rock** with burbling springs and lush plant life; nice views from the top.

To Get There

This trail is located inside Lory State Park, a 19.5-mile drive from downtown Fort Collins. To reach the park, take Mulberry Street west to Overland Trail Road and turn north. Drive 2.5 miles along curvy Overland Trail to Bingham Hill Road and turn left (headed west). Continue until the stop sign at Bellvue. Turn left at the T, and you'll see a sign posted to Lory State Park. You'll notice another park sign steering you right onto CR 25G just before the northernmost dam of Horsetooth Reservoir. Drive on CR 25G to the park's boundary, being sure to stop at the visitor center to pay your $5 daily fee.

To reach the Well Gulch trailhead, continue down the gravel road past the Timber trailhead. If you reach the picnic area, you've gone too far. Parking is available across the road from the trailhead.

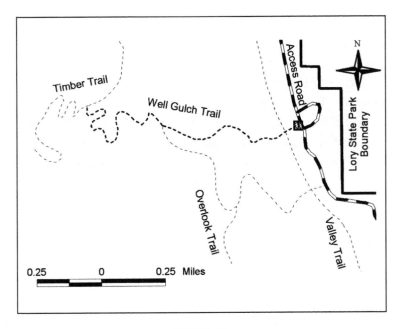

Well Gulch

The Hike

You may want to obtain the Well Gulch interpretive brochure before leaving the visitor center. As you walk the trail, you'll find several stations that identify plant and animal species and give geological tidbits about the area.

This lush walk takes you into a deep gulch just north of **Arthur's Rock**. From the parking area, it is possible to look up at the gorge you are about to explore. Sheltered by ponderosa pines and cooled by the creek, Well Gulch is a good choice on a hot summer day. Walk past the trailhead sign along a sandy trail and into the dark shadows of the rock walls of the canyon. Unlike the walls of Arthur's Rock, which are formed from pegmatite, the canyon walls of Well Gulch are a black schist. The trail very soon encounters a small seeping water pool, which the schist rock cliffs encircle protectively. A lovely spot. From here, the trail goes deeper into the lush foliage before emerging onto sunny, grassy meadows fringed by massive cottonwoods.

Your hike becomes more strenuous where the trail begins to climb as it carves into the mountainside. Soon it ventures out onto the south-facing hillside to switchback up to the Timber Trail connection where the Well Gulch Trail ends. I suggest extending the length of the walk by taking the left fork south for fine views of the sandstone hogbacks and Horsetooth Reservoir below. Here some of the pine trees, straying from their cool forest onto the rocky, sun-beaten hillside, grow in strange, bonsai-like shapes. The trail winds back around into the north side of the draw where the contrast of life zones is stark: You will see mosses drooping from the Douglas firs and Engelmann spruce. The Timber Trail continues several miles into some of the more remote regions of the state park.

LOVELAND/BIG THOMPSON AREA

Provided here is a sampling of the hikes to be found in and around Loveland and the Big Thompson Canyon. Although no hikes are included inside Rocky Mountain National Park in this section of the book (many other guides can be found dedicated solely to that purpose), both **Round Mountain** and **Crosier Mountain** take you right up to the window of the park for some of the best views into the area to be found anywhere.

I am also happy to be able to provide information on a brand-new natural area on the outskirts of Loveland. **Devils Backbone** was a landmark begging to be opened to the public.

Crosier Mountain

▶ 5.75 miles one way   ▶ Strenuous

Maps: U.S.G.S. Glen Haven

Beginning Elevation: 6,400 feet

Ending Elevation: 9,250 feet

Access Road: Paved county road

Season: Early summer to fall

Connector Trails: There are three accesses to Crosier Mountain's summit. All are discussed here.

Highlights: This hike leads up through a diversity of life zones—meadows, creek draws, quiet conifer forests—to a rocky summit for views of Rocky Mountain National Park.

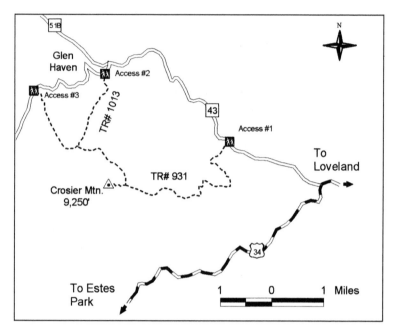

Crosier Mountain

To Get There

From Fort Collins, take Taft Hill Road to Loveland. At the junction with Highway 34, go right up Big Thompson Canyon 13 miles to Drake. At the Glen Haven turnoff onto CR 43 (or Devils Gulch Road), go right. It is 2 miles to *Access #1*, which can be identified by a gate on the left at the bottom of a small knoll with a small parking area available. *Access #2* is 5.5 miles up CR 43. A road sign points out the trailhead at one end of a large parking lot. *Access #3* is 8 miles up CR 43 at the town of Glen Haven. The trailhead is located on the upper outskirts of town.

The Hike

Access #1 is probably the most picturesque of the three with an unusual grassy meadow that blooms in wildflowers midsummer. *Access*

At a lookout point near the summit of Crosier Mountain

#3 from Glen Haven offers the most views of Rocky Mountain National Park and is considered the easiest ascent. *Access #2* provides the best parking and climbs through some lovely forest, however steeply.

From *Access #1*, climb Trail #931 up over the small knoll onto a grassy meadow and into ponderosa and juniper forest along a small drainage. Switchbacks soon tighten as the path makes its way up to the large open meadow, a destination in itself for those interested in a shorter hike (1.5 miles). The meadow sits like a bench above Glen Haven Canyon, overshadowed at one end by an unnamed peak. Past the meadow, the trail ascends through the rocks to a ridge from which you can view the devastation of the Drake fire of 2000. The path winds through fire-scorched patches, passing the charred skeletons of pines. From here, follow the trail as it drops into a gorge. Exciting geology looms overhead as the trail again climbs. This section of trail is somewhat crumbly because it is crowded on one side by stone and the other by an intermittent stream that feeds the aspens growing along it. The upper reaches of the trail traverse ponderosa pine meadows with views of Crosier Mountain ahead. At 5 miles, you will encounter a trail junction; straight ahead leads to *Accesses #2* and *#3*. Turn left, following the path 0.75 mile to access the summit. The last leg is rough but short. At the high point, a rocky pinnacle affords views of Rocky Mountain National Park and Estes Park. The rocks have been shaped and hollowed by the wind that often howls up here. A beautiful Douglas fir grows on the edge of the cliff, its massive roots exposed as it hangs on for dear life. Explore a bit while you're up here. You'll find multiple lookout points and rock outcroppings.

Accesses #2 and *#3* make their way to the summit from the north and northwest. *Access #2*, known as Trail #1013, begins to climb immediately from the parking area, switchbacking most of the way. This side of the mountain, along both the Glen Haven and #1013 Trails, is dominated by dark ponderosa pine forest, wild currant, and wildflowers flourishing in its understory. As the forest opens out where the two trails meet, mammoth aspens and Douglas firs create an expansive ambience. Watch for an impressive dead snag on the downhill slope just below the #1013/ Glen Haven junction. From here the two trails join to climb moderately up through immature lodgepole pine forest to the junction with Trail #931 and the summit trail. Both #1013 and the Glen Haven Trails reach the summit at 4.75 miles. To do an easy combination of these hikes, use a two-car shuttle, leaving a second vehicle at one of the other trailheads and hiking over the mountain to it.

Devils Backbone Nature Trail

▶ 3.75 miles round-trip   ▶ Easy

Maps: U.S.G.S. Loveland

Beginning Elevation: 5,080 feet

Ending Elevation: 5,250 feet

Access Road: Good gravel road last 700 feet, all cars

Season: Year-round, depending on weather

Connector Trails: Blue Sky Trail

Highlights: Natural area just outside Loveland city limits with fascinating rock formations, a perfect choice for the whole family.

To Get There

From Fort Collins, take Taft Hill Road out of town south to the city of Loveland. At the T junction, turn right (west) onto Highway 34, the one toward Estes Park. You will be able to see "the backbone" to the north. Just before you pass the "backbone," turn right at the Devil's Backbone Trail sign. This is also the access road to Hidden Valley Estates. Follow the road into a large parking area. The trail starts just beyond the restrooms.

The Hike

In 1998, a geological treasure in the Loveland foothills became part of the natural-areas program and opened to the public in 1999. Devils Backbone is an unusual rock formation visible from many places in the city, but to walk the length of it is a real treat.

The "hogbacks," as they are known, which stretch from north of Fort Collins all the way down the Front Range and including Devils Backbone,

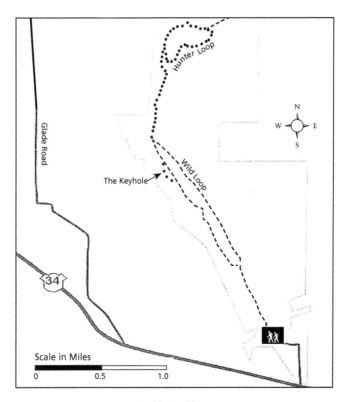

Devils Backbone

are remnants of an ancient seafloor that has been exposed by wind and water over hundreds of thousands of years. Indeed, the hogbacks are more ancient than the Rocky Mountains themselves. Pawnee Buttes, which are 75 miles away, are also remnants of the ancient seabed.

The trail drops down into a cottonwood grove where picnic tables sit in a cool shade. The trail is dear to the hearts of equestrians and mountain bikers alike, and you'll want to keep an eye out for oncoming traffic. You can do the loop as an interpretive nature walk by obtaining a leaflet from a box along the trail. Spring is a lovely time to visit: The early

The "windows" at Devils Backbone

wildflowers are beginning to unfold, and the yellow mountain mahogany and blue flax are standing in vivid contrast to the dark, severe rocks.

To enjoy the interpretive trail, do the loop in a clockwise fashion, staying on the high road for the best views of the windows, eyes, and arches chiseled from the stone by the forces of wind and weather. It is interesting to imagine the formation as it might have been millennia ago, or how it might be altered in the future in the blink of a geological eye. The cliffs are home to many nesting birds. During my visit in May, the branch trail up to the largest hole in the rock was closed off to protect a raven's nest from human disturbance, a request that I was happy to oblige.

The trail loops back on itself at 1.75 miles, dropping down to a lower level where views of the backbone are limited. However, the vistas of the red hogbacks to the east are splendid, especially at sunset. Numerous birds of many species inhabit the mahogany-brush hills, and it's worth bringing along a pair of binoculars.

At the far end of the loop, you can choose to extend the length of your walk by continuing up the ridge to reach the Hunter's Loop. This section of the trail is quite strenuous. From the top you're rewarded with marvelous views into Rocky Mountain National Park. The upper arm of the loop is open only to foot traffic while the lower section is open to horses and bikes as well. Beyond the Hunter's Loop, the trail connects with the Laughing Horse Loop and the **Blue Sky Trail** and can be used to hike the entire length of the hogbacks between Loveland and Fort Collins!

Return to the parking area the way you came.

Round Mountain

▶ **4.75 miles round-trip**   ▶ **Strenuous**

Maps: U.S.G.S. Drake

Beginning Elevation: 5,960 feet

Ending Elevation: 7,480 feet

Access Road: Paved highway

Season: Early summer to fall

Connector Trails: Round Mountain Interpretive Loop

Highlights: A hard hike above the Big Thompson River through

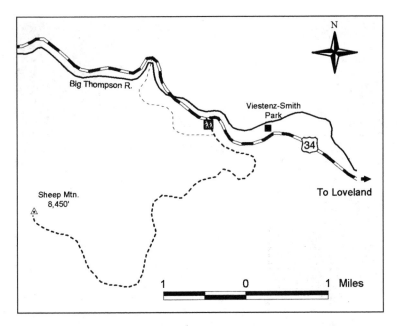

Round Mountain

unearthly rock outcroppings to the top of a mountain for
wonderful views.

To Get There

From Fort Collins, take Taft Hill Road to Loveland. At the T junction,
turn right (west) onto Highway 34 toward Estes Park. Continue about 5
miles up Big Thompson Canyon to the trailhead parking on the left just
beyond Viestenz-Smith Picnic Area, which is on the right.

The Hike

From the parking area, walk past the restrooms up a wide gravel
road. The first 0.25 mile overlaps with the easy 1 mile interpretive trail,

A unique slot on the Round Mountain Trail

so even if you intend to do the Summit Trail, it's worth picking up a leaflet at the trailhead.

The two trails split, clearly marked at the fork. The Summit Trail immediately begins climbing along a route parallel to the Big Thompson River and the highway, visible below. The trail doesn't pretend to choose its route carefully but instead switchbacks at a knee-buckling climb up the mountainside. Bring an extra water bottle for each member of the party, and plan on making it a daylong hike. The trail is only 4.75 miles, but every inch is straight up. You will climb through Douglas firs primarily but also will see ponderosas, wild currant, mountain mahogany, and a great assortment of wildflowers. The Summit Trail also serves as an interpretive trail, with several information plaques posted (nicely spaced for just when you need a breather).

Once the trail reaches the top of the canyon wall, it breaks out onto open hillsides that can get quite sun-beaten in the summer. At the 2-mile marker, the views of the plains offer horizons that must be 80 miles distant. From here, it is still impossible to see Round Mountain's summit.

Soon the terrain is dominated by granite boulders and Stonehenge-like beauty of the rock-encrusted eastern flank of Round Mountain. Aspens growing among the rocks give the area a particularly special feel.

A great spot to sit and enjoy the outdoors comes at a small spring seeping out of the mountainside near the 3-mile marker. The last 1.75 miles offers views of Round Mountain's round top, but this summit is not where you are headed. The trail takes you to the top of tree-covered Sheep Mountain. Follow rock cairns the final leg up to the grassy summit. The views of Long's Peak and the Continental Divide are worth the extra distance. However, the boulder field and the spring at the 3-mile point are rewarding destinations in themselves.

Pawnee National Grasslands

You can't say you've really seen Colorado until you've visited the Pawnee Buttes on the eastern plains. Recently, it has become a pilgrimage destination for many people who appreciate the ethereal beauty of the prairie with its constantly changing light and haunting birdcalls. Although lots of folks come for the mountain biking potential, mountain bikes are not allowed on the trail to the Pawnee Buttes but are restricted to outlying dirt roads.

The Pawnee Buttes are named after a tribe of Native Americans who sometimes frequented the area but usually lived on the grasslands of Nebraska and Kansas. The Pawnee were an unusual plains tribe in that they engaged not only in hunting but also in an agrarian lifestyle, raising corn, beans, and squash along the river bottoms.

Many other plains tribes, including the Arapaho, Cheyenne, and Sioux, also visited Pawnee Buttes and hunted buffalo and antelope here. According to legend, a battle ensued here between the Pawnee and the Sioux. The Pawnee were not known as warriors, but the Sioux practiced an elaborate warrior code of conduct reminiscent of medieval Europe. The Sioux forced the Pawnee up onto the east butte and trapped them there without food or water. However, once night had fallen and the Sioux let down their guard, one Pawnee warrior was able to escape down a rope made of horsehair ropes tied end to end. He carved footholds down the precipice for the others, and they slipped away through the maze of ravines to the east. People say the footholds are still visible on the northwest side of the butte.

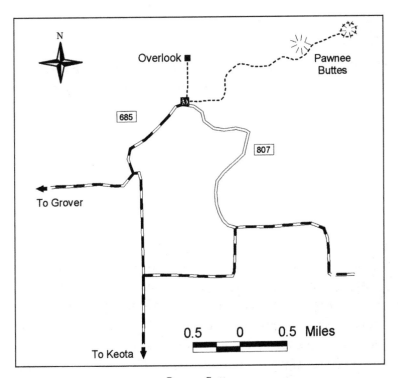

Pawnee Buttes

16 Pawnee Buttes

▶ 2.5 miles round-trip ▶ Easy

Maps: U.S.G.S. Pawnee Buttes

Beginning Elevation: 5,300 feet

Ending Elevation: 5,200 feet

Access Road: Good gravel road last 15 miles

Season: Year-round, depending on weather

Connector Trails: None

Highlights: One of the most unusual trails described in this book, a walk across the prairie to fascinating sandstone buttes, great views of the prairie and the distant mountains, good opportunities to view prairie wildlife.

To Get There

This hike is located 65 miles east of Fort Collins out onto the plains. From downtown Fort Collins, take Mulberry Street east to the I–25 overpass where Mulberry becomes Highway 14 east.

The drive to get to the Pawnee Buttes is as rewarding as the hike itself. Drive 13 miles to Ault on Highway 14 east and on through Briggsdale, where a shady campground is available on the north side of the highway (road signs are posted). Continue on Highway 14 to the Keota turnoff where a "Pawnee National Grasslands" sign is posted. This route is well marked at each of the numerous road forks. Other routes are not so easy to follow.

Keep a good road map handy. Just before reaching the buttes, you pass through Keota, an old-timey semi–ghost town in the middle of the prairie with views of the bluffs you're headed for.

At the intersection where signs point to the buttes in both directions, continue straight to the trailhead road and then turn right at the Pawnee National Grasslands sign. The last mile uphill to the trailhead can get deeply rutted, and you may need a high-clearance vehicle for this stretch, depending on weather conditions. The trailhead is on the left after a windmill. Road #807 makes a loop back to the main access road and provides good camping spots with vistas of the buttes. A portable toilet is available at the trailhead.

View of West Pawnee Butte

The Hike

Two trails launch off from the parking area. The Overlook Trail stays along the bluff's ridge to a lookout point with vertigo-inspiring views from the tops of the high white cliffs. This trail is closed to visitors March 1 to June 30 for the protection of nesting raptors. However, springtime is when the Pawnee Buttes are seen at their best. The wildflowers and cactus are blooming, the birds are frolicking, and the heat is less oppressive. In midsummer, the prairie can get dangerously hot if you aren't prepared with plenty of water.

To walk to the buttes, follow a foot path down onto a grassy plateau where views of the white cliffs of Lips Bluff open out below you. The forces of wind and water have molded the soft stone into unearthly shapes, and the trail leads you down among them as the prairie floor gives way to the sculpting hand of water. As you round the bluffs, the two monolithic shapes of the Pawnee Buttes come into view. The trail takes you to the foot of the first butte's sheer wall of pinkish stone. You can't imagine the buttes' immensity until you're in their shadows. Both the west and east buttes are made of a very soft sandstone that is not recommended for rock climbing. Like the hogbacks of the Front Range, the Pawnee Buttes are the exposed remains of an ancient sea bottom that predates the Rocky Mountains.

Between the west and east buttes, the trail crosses onto private property, and the east butte lies almost completely outside the Pawnee National Grasslands except for its south flank. This means no camping or campfires. The west butte is inaccessible, but the east butte (5,375 feet) does have a crumbly foot path that leads around its perimeter for views from above of the wrinkled ravine prairie floor and opportunities to spot soaring raptors and to undertake self-guided explorations of the area. After making the loop around the east butte, return to the parking area the way you came.

RED FEATHER LAKES

The Red Feather Lakes area, located northwest of Fort Collins, is a large tract of mother nature that offers fascinating hiking potential through a wild granite-strewn landscape spotted with reflective pools and lakes. Red Feather Lakes sits above Poudre Canyon to the north, draining the North Fork of the Cache la Poudre River. The area can be accessed from a scenic alternate route from Rustic that takes you through the old town site of Manhattan, the hub of Larimer County's own little gold rush. There isn't much to see at the road junction of FR 162 and FR 68C, but much of Red Feather's history sprang up around the old ghost town. Catherine Lawder came to Manhattan in 1883 and later married Frank B. Gartman, who worked in the gold mines for $1 a day while she did the washing for people of the community. When an English gentleman named Cecil Moon became ill, Mrs. Gartman nursed him back to health and, in the end, obtained a divorce from her husband and married her patient. Cecil later inherited the title of baron and became Sir Cecil Moon. Catherine became Lady Moon and is a well-known Red Feather character, the namesake of many landmarks.

Red Feather Lakes is named for Princess Tsianina, a Cherokee/ Creek songstress whose name meant Red Feather. She toured France and America and made a stopover to perform for this out-of-the-way community, whose residents were so enchanted by her voice and charm that they named their corner of the globe for her and for the red feather she always wore in her hair.

Red Feather Lakes is surrounded by Roosevelt National Forest. Many trails are multiple-use, and trekkers can sometimes expect to encounter ATVs (all-terrain vehicles). All trails are open to mountain bikes unless otherwise noted at the trailhead. Red Feather Lakes Village provides most modern conveniences. (See the "Red Feather Services" section at the back of this book to obtain contact information concerning groceries, RV parks, and more.)

Eagle's Nest Rock

▶ 4.75 miles round-trip   ▶ Moderate

Maps: Livermore

Beginning Elevation: 6000 feet

Ending Elevation: 5700 feet

Access Road: Good gravel road last 1.25 miles

Distance Round Trip: 4.75 miles

Difficulty: Moderate

Season: Spring to fall

Connector Trails: OT Trail and 3-Bar Trail connect, forming a barbell-shaped trail.

Highlights: Unique destination to a new open space area with lovely geology and opportunities for raptor sightings and fishing.

To Get There

From Ted's Place (junction of 287 and 14), take Highway 287 north toward Laramie to the Twin Forks turn-off at Livermore on CR 74E. Drive through the town of Livermore about 0.25 mile to the Eagle's Nest Rock sign located just past the fire station and turn left here. Follow this good gravel road as it curves up to the trailhead. Restrooms are available at the parking lot.

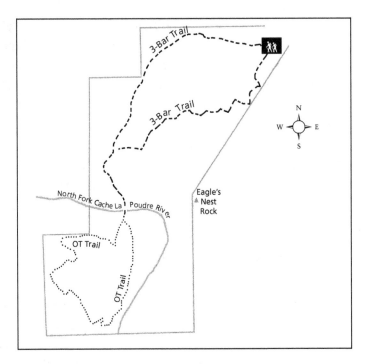

Eagle's Nest Rock

The Hike

As I was setting out on my hike, I was lucky enough to make the acquaintance of a park ranger who gave me an explanation for this new open space's name. He pointed out a prominent knob visible to the south of the trailhead where he said eagles nest each year in a crevice off the upper cliffs of the landmark. Although I kept my eye on that crevice the entire duration of my visit, I never did see a circling bird of prey. Hopefully others after me will be luckier.

I chose to do my hike in a clockwise route but there is no advantage in making the loop in one direction or another; either way the hike is moderately strenuous with only a couple of a hard but short stretches of trail. In a clockwise direction, the 3-Bar Trail stays always in the shadow of Eagle's Nest Rock, traversing mahogany brush hillsides, musical with birds. There are no shade trees along the trail and you'll want to bring along plenty of water if visiting during the heat of summer. Also note that the hike explores rattlesnake country. A good pair of ankle-high boots is always a good idea at this elevation. The trail contours in and out of numerous draws with great views of the rock (although that crevice doesn't come clearly into view until you reach the river) before dropping steeply down into the valley floor where cottonwoods provide shade for wandering cattle. Watch the trail posts carefully, veering away from the "No Public Access" signs and following the rust metal posts directing you up and over a low ridge to the river.

At the bridge spanning the North Fork of the Cache La Poudre River, you'll find a great place to seek shade under an aromatic ponderosa or narrow-leaf cottonwood with a perfect screen to sit and watch for raptors hunting above you. A hitching post is provided here for folks on horseback. Or you might choose to bring along a fishing rod to explore a cobbled stretch of historic river. Several famous trappers and explorers such as John Frémont and Kit Carson used the North Fork of the Cache La Poudre as their primary route into the North Platte and Laramie River regions.

The river's edge makes a perfect trail destination, and marks the end of the 3-Bar Loop, but you may continue on to the OT (oh-tee) Trail, looping around another 1.75 miles if you're interested in extending your time in this lovely country. Cross the wide boardwalk bridge and pass through the gate, being sure to close it behind you, following an old ranch road through meadows recently re-seeded and cordoned off with electric fencing (a vivid reminder to follow the rules and keep dogs on leashes). At the farthest reaches of the OT Loop, watch for views of a recent burn that scorched the entire hillside to the south. Soon the OT Trail climbs up onto a sometimes gusty ridge where National Forest can be accessed via an overgrown road that beacons into wild country.

Upon returning to the bridge, retrace your steps back along the 3-Bar Trail and return to the parking area along the other arm of your loop. On my clockwise trip, I found the western curve of the loop a bit confusing as the single-track trail turned to double track. The last leg up to my car was a strenuous workout.

Killpecker Creek Trail #956

▶ 3.25 miles one way   ▶ Moderate

Maps: U.S.G.S. South Bald Mountain

Beginning Elevation: 9,163 feet

Ending Elevation: 10,700 feet

Access Road: Medium-grade gravel road

Season: Early summer to fall

Connector Trails: North Lone Pine Trail #953

Highlights: Alternate route to Middle Bald Mountain along a wide, often roaring creek with several small waterfalls.

To Get There

From Ted's Place (junction of 287 and 14), take Highway 287 north (toward Laramie) to the Twin Forks turnoff onto CR 74E to Red Feather Lakes. Continue on this paved road past the turnoff to the Red Feather Lakes Village. Soon after, the pavement ends, and the road becomes

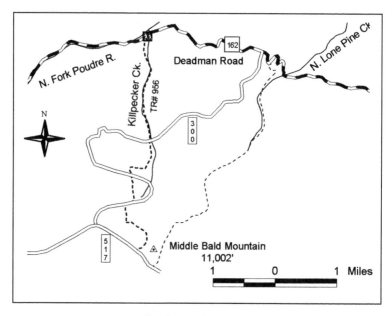

Killpecker Creek Trail #956

the rather rough CR 162 (Deadman Road). Take this road past the **North Lone Pine** trailhead. The road traverses the site of the 1978 Killpecker fire, which was the result of human negligence and burned 1,200 acres. The Killpecker Creek trailhead and a small parking area are located just down the road from the entrance to the North Fork Poudre Campground.

The Hike

This hike makes a great loop or two-car shuttle in connection with the North Lone Pine Trail. If you decide to make a loop of it, you will have to walk the last few miles along Deadman Road. The Killpecker Trail section of the loop is open to motorcycles but isn't used much for this purpose. I visited on the Sunday of Memorial Day weekend and encountered no motorcycles during my hike.

One of the many waterfalls along Killpecker Creek

From the trailhead, walk past the informational display sign and into a dense lodgepole pine and Engelmann spruce forest. Until the 0.5-mile point, you can hear but not see Killpecker Creek. In the late spring, the creek fills its banks in a white torrent. There are two creek crossings over log footbridges, but even when the water is high, they aren't unduly nerve-wracking. The trail maintains a close neighborliness with the creek for the first 2 miles, providing plenty of chances to see small-to-midsize waterfalls as they carry the mountain runoff down to meet the North Fork of the Poudre River. The two bodies of water come together near the trailhead. (During the earliest explorations of the Front Range area, many famous trappers and explorers such as John Fremont and Kit Carson used the North Fork of the Cache la Poudre as their primary route into the North Platte and Laramie River regions.)

The path can get difficult to keep track of where it weaves through rocky terrain, but the way is well posted if you watch for trail blazes slashed into the tree trunks (they look like upside-down exclamation marks).

At 2 miles, the trail veers away from the creek drainage and plateaus, crossing through an immature pine forest to meet a road (FR 300). At the road, walk to the left about 500 feet to a rock cairn (rock pile) on the other side and continue up the trail. The path again intersects FR 300 soon after. At 3 miles, the trail climbs out onto 4WD road 517. Turn left here and walk east 0.25 mile until the road climbs up to a saddle. The views at the saddle make Middle Bald Mountain seem close enough to touch. Anyone interested in seeing the world from the top can reach the mountain summit from this point. Middle Bald Mountain is a long rock-encrusted ridge with multiple false peaks.

To make a loop of the trail with the North Lone Pine Trail, continue 0.25 mile down the 4WD road to a large rock cairn on the left.

19 Mount Margaret

▶ 4 miles one way ▶ Easy

Maps: U.S.G.S. Red Feather Lakes

Beginning Elevation: 8,093 feet

Ending Elevation: 7,957 feet

Access Road: Paved road

Season: Year-round, depending on weather

Connector Trails: Dowdy Lake Trail, Loop A and B trails

Highlights: Quintessential Red Feather: wildflower meadows,

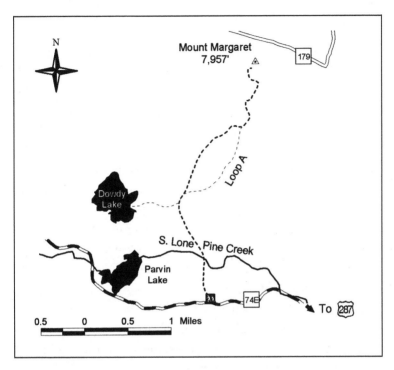

Mount Margaret

ponderosa pines, aspens, a pond, and, of course, unusual rocks. The views from the summit aren't bad either.

To Get There

From Ted's Place (junction of 287 and 14), take Highway 287 north toward Laramie to the Twin Forks turnoff on CR 74E to Red Feather Lakes. The trailhead is 20 miles from the Twin Forks turnoff. Just before reaching the Roosevelt National Forest boundary and Parvin Lake, you will see a small pull-out parking area on the side of the road and the trailhead sign behind a large gate. There is no road sign designating the trailhead.

The Hike

From the trailhead, go through the gate and follow the old dirt track as it crosses the first of many large grassy meadows where the wildflowers in summer grow in abundance. The entire walk offers panoramic views of the Red Feather region and its strange rock-strewn landscape, a beautiful place that the Mount Margaret Trail captures at its best. At a creek crossing, it may be necessary to backtrack on a side path about 200 yards to a footbridge invisible for all the willow bushes. Because the walk provides little shade in the first mile, be sure to bring ample water. The forest is equal parts ponderosa pine and aspen, a lovely combination. Corridors through the aspens lead out onto bizarre vistas of unnamed rock formations. Some of the rocks are like funky sculpture. Just when you are wondering what the artist was thinking, you remember that the artist was mother nature.

The Mount Margaret trail system draws many mountain bikers, providing many dirt roads branching off, the next destination better than the last. There is ample room for everyone on the wide trail as long as all visitors respect the rights of others.

Just past a large gate, the dirt tracks fork. Stay straight on FR 307. At a second fork, wooden signs point the direction to Dowdy Lake for those interested in a backdoor route to the lake. The Loop Trail A also veers off from this junction. By taking the loop, you can extend your mileage to Mount Margaret by 1.25 miles and enjoy close-up views along a fascinating rocky ridge.

Beyond the fork, you now are on a beeline for Mount Margaret. All along the trail, I kept eyeing each rock-capped mountain I passed, wondering, is that the one I'm searching for? Or this one? Mount Margaret isn't visible until you're at its summit. Where the loop returns to the Mount Margaret Trail is a lovely circular pond, overgrown with reeds; this is a nice spot to sit and spy on the red-winged blackbirds that flock there.

From the summit of Mount Margaret

The dirt road soon narrows to a single track, and without even realizing it, you begin to climb a short gentle ridge to the summit. At the top, look north to the vistas of the cathedral-spire rocks that cast their shadows over the green valley. You're in for more views when you scale the rocks to Mount Margaret's summit. The large horseshoe-shaped terrain below is the result of glaciation in the ancient ice age that shaped much of Colorado's high country.

There is abundant exploring to be done in the Mount Margaret/ Dowdy Lake trail system, by foot or mountain bike. See the informational display at the trailhead for more ideas. Multiple campsites with numbered posts are available along the entire stretch of the Mount Margaret Trail, including a deluxe site located at the pond.

North Lone Pine Trail #953

▶ 5.25 miles one way   ▶ Moderate

Maps: U.S.G.S. South Bald Mountain

Beginning Elevation: 9,474 feet

Ending Elevation: 11,002 feet

Access Road: Medium-grade gravel road last 4 miles

Season: Early summer to fall

Connector Trails: Killpecker Creek Trail, Swamp Creek Cutoff Trail

Highlights: Creek-side trek featuring several small waterfalls with the option at the end to climb a "bald" mountain for views of surrounding Red Feather area.

To Get There

From Ted's Place (junction of 287 and 14), take Highway 287 north toward Laramie to the Twin Forks turnoff onto CR 74E to Red Feather Lakes. Continue on this paved road past the turnoff to Red Feather Lakes Village. Soon after, the pavement ends, and the road becomes the increasingly rough CR 162 (Deadman Road). Take it 4 miles to the North Lone Pine trailhead and overlook. Picnic tables and a large parking area are available.

The Hike

The North Lone Pine Trail was originally a stock drive trail used by local ranchers to herd cattle into the high country. In 1979, the trail was reconstructed for hiking access into the three Bald Mountains area, North, Middle, and South.

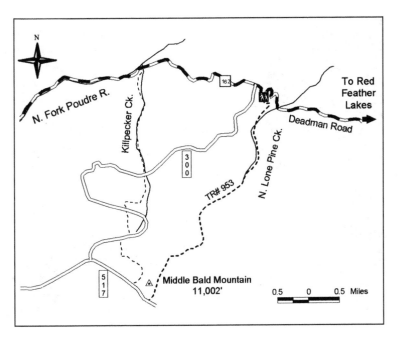

North Lone Pine Trail #953

From the trailhead, you will maintain an easy climb through lodgepole pine and Douglas fir stands. The trail soon takes you into aspen groves, spruces, and subalpine firs. At 1 mile, you will hear the roar of a multitiered waterfall. The trail continues to climb along the creek side, crossing a logging road near several visible clear-cuts at the 2-mile point. Locate the rock cairn directly across the road and keep going, encountering the road a second time only a few hundred yards later where you again cross directly over, following rock cairns.

After the road crossings, the path traverses boulder fields in mile 3. The trail is obscured, and it is often necessary to follow cairns and trail blazes in the trees (blazes look like upside-down exclamation marks). Trail blazes are seldom used to mark trails today because they open the tree to infections that can eventually kill it and cause the spread of disease

Middle Bald Mountain's summit

throughout an entire stand of trees. The trail reaches a densely wooded plateau, then follows the terrain as it curves around toward South and Middle Bald Mountains. (By this point, the trail has already bypassed North Bald Mountain without any clear views.) A large rock outcropping on the left (east) near the end of the trail provides views of South Bald Mountain and an especially good silhouette of Middle Bald Mountain.

At 5 miles, the trail abruptly T's at an intersection with 4WD road #517. The road is marked with orange metal plates posted on the trees. To reach the Swamp Creek Cutoff Trail and South Bald Mountain, go left (east) on FR 517. To reach Middle Bald Mountain or to make a loop of the hike by accessing the Killpecker Creek Trail, go right (west) on the 4WD road. Expect to encounter ATVs (all-terrain vehicles) and motorbikes using this road also. After walking a short 0.25 mile up the road, you will be at a saddle with radical views of Middle Bald Mountain from its very foot. From this saddle, it is possible to climb Middle Bald Mountain by scrambling up its talus slope. Middle Bald Mountain is more of a long ridge than a proper peak. Expect to encounter false peaks as you climb to its highest point for a vantage of the surrounding area. Bring a topographical map and have the satisfaction of identifying your landmarks. As is true of most summits, the winds can be extreme, so I recommend bringing extra layers of clothing.

To make a loop or two-car shuttle of the hike, access the Killpecker Creek Trail from the base of Middle Bald Mountain by continuing west another 0.25 mile on FR 517 to the trail intersection. Keep in mind that making a loop of the hike requires walking a few miles back to your car along Deadman Road.

Around Town

In the 1990s, the city of Fort Collins looked into the future and saw that its rapidly developing community would soon overtake its natural spaces if steps weren't initiated to preserve them. The City of Fort Collins Natural Areas System continues today to designate wetlands, prairie grasslands, foothills, and wildlife riparian lands as part of the city's heritage. Most of the walks and hiking included in this section pertain to the city's natural areas. Many of them are interconnected by city bike routes or by longer trails such as the Foothills Trail that consists of three shorter trails: Pineridge, Maxwell, and Campeau Natural Area Trails. City employees maintain and patrol the parks by mountain bike and do issue tickets for dogs without leashes. For further information on each area's regulations, see signs posted at trailheads. And watch for new natural areas to open up in the future. Here's a hint: The city designates natural areas by bordering them with buck-and-rail fence, something to watch for if you're like me, always looking for a new spot to explore.

21 Blue Sky Trail

▶ **9.75 miles one way**   ▶ **Moderate**

Maps: Horsetooth Reservoir, Masonville, Loveland

Beginning Elevation: 6,000 feet

Ending Elevation: 5,500 feet

Access Road: Good gravel road, all cars

Season: Year round, depending on weather

Connector Trails: Rimrock Trail; **Devil's Backbone; Coyote Ridge Trail**; Indian Summer Trail

Highlights: Recently completed trail down a valley between two ridges of the foothills that can be used to link Horsetooth Reservoir to Loveland with options for shorter excursions.

To Get There

This trail can be accessed from the Devil's Backbone, Coyote Ridge or the Soderberg trailheads. Since the first two are listed elsewhere in this book, the description here will give driving directions to the Soderberg Trailhead.

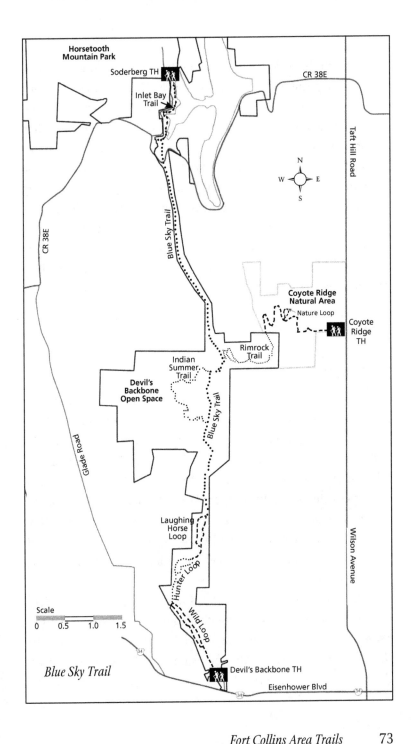

Horsetooth
Mountain Park

Soderberg TH

Inlet Bay
Trail

CR 38E

CR 38E

Taft Hill Road

Blue Sky Trail

N
W E
S

Coyote Ridge
Natural Area

Nature Loop

Coyote
Ridge
TH

Rimrock
Trail

Indian
Summer
Trail

Devil's
Backbone
Open Space

Blue Sky Trail

Glade Road

Laughing
Horse
Loop

Hunter Loop

Wild Loop

Wilson Avenue

Scale

0   0.5   1.0   1.5

Blue Sky Trail

Devil's Backbone TH

Eisenhower Blvd

To reach the Soderberg parking lot from downtown Fort Collins, take Mulberry Street west to Taft Hill Road and head south to Harmony Street. At this intersection, turn right (west) on CR 38E and take it around Horsetooth Reservoir to Shoreline Drive. At the intersection of CR 38E and Shoreline Drive, you'll see a fire station and a brown recreation sign for Inlet Bay and the boat launch. Follow Shoreline Drive as it winds past a large boat parking lot and a campground on the right. The Soderberg Trailhead is on your left with a restroom available at the parking lot.

The Blue Sky Trail makes a perfect two-car shuttle excursion. Leave a vehicle at one of the other trailheads and bike or hike your way from a second trailhead over to get it. In my case, I started at the Soderberg TH and biked to the Devil's Backbone TH. This seemed to be a popular choice for mountain bikers, but a hiker might choose explore the slightly shorter distance (7.75 miles) to Coyote Ridge.

The Hike/Ride

Two trails head off from this parking area, one north 5.5 miles to Lory State Park and the other south to intersect the Rimrock Trail. To reach the Blue Sky Trail, pick up a trail on the opposite side of the road as it crosses through the campground. The first 1.25 mile is named the Inlet Bay Trail although it seamlessly joins the Blue Sky Trail as it passes under the highway. The Inlet Bay Trail section is mostly a wide improved gravel route, although it turns to a narrow unimproved path just before the underpass. After dipping under the highway, the path opens out, nothing between you and Loveland but rock and sky (okay, and a big house on every bluff!).

Although there are very few trails in this guide of which I didn't walk each and every mile, I chose to mountain bike the Blue Sky Trail because of its distance. I must admit that I saw very few hikers along the first two-thirds of the trail. Most pedestrians and horses seem to stick to the Coyote Ridge and Devil's Backbone areas, leaving the Blue Sky Trail

Along the Blue Sky Trail

for the mountain bikers. The trail is narrow, making it necessary to share the trail carefully, mountain bikers yielding to both hikers and horses (and hikers should yield to horses). Because of the volume of mountain bikes on the trail, some sections of the trail are powdery, causing tricky footing and riding. An astonishing magenta sandstone rimrock juts out against the blue sky above you as you follow the backside of the eastern ridge of the foothills through yucca and rabbitbrush. The trail can be exceptionally hot with little to no shade in the summertime. A good choice might be to investigate this trail during the autumn when the cottonwoods and mountain mahogany brush turn shades to take your breath away. Keep in mind, with lots of rock alcoves and prairie dog towns, this is also prime rattler country.

At about 4.25 miles you reach the Rimrock Trail intersection. Those folks headed east to the Coyote Ridge Trailhead should turn off here. The rest should continue following the trail as it drops down into the valley bottom, crossing a dry creek bed where a cool resting spot can be found near a cottonwood grove. Soon after the grove, you'll intersect the Indian Summer Trail, a 2 mile side loop that gives you access to the western slope of the foothills. Meanwhile, the Blue Sky Trail continues, clearly marked as it switches to double track and back again. A bench under a cottonwood makes a great place to nap the heat of the day away.

Immediately after this rest area, the trail climbs up to ride the top of the ridge via a series of reinforced bridges stair-stepping up the rocky incline. The Blue Sky Trail ends when it reaches the Laughing Horse Loop (the mileage I've listed however is from trailhead to trailhead). Only hikers and horses are allowed on the western side of the Laughing Horse, Hunter and Wild Loops, requiring that mountain bikes stick to the eastern arms of these loops.

The ride gets much more technical on the rim top, the hiking more slippery, but the views into Rocky Mountain National Park also seem to hover just outside your touch. In this southern section of the trail system, development encroaches into the valley below. After the Hunter Loop, the trail drops steeply down behind the Devil's Backbone formation. Expect to encounter much more foot, horse and bike traffic the closer you get to Devil's Backbone, a popular destination for outdoor enthusiasts of every stripe. At the new Devil's Backbone parking area you'll get one last opportunity to relax in the shade of a cottonwood.

Campeau Natural Area

▶ 2.25 miles one way   ▶ Moderate

Maps: U.S.G.S. Fort Collins

Beginning Elevation: 5,080 feet

Ending Elevation: 5,320 feet

Access Road: Paved street, all cars

Season: Year-round, depending on weather

Connector Trails: Foothills Trail connecting to **Maxwell** and **Pineridge** trailheads

Highlights: Of the three Foothills Trail sections, Campeau has the wildest feel, boasting interesting rock formations, views into the Bellvue Valley area, and possibilities for self-guided explorations.

The footbridge at the Campeau trailhead

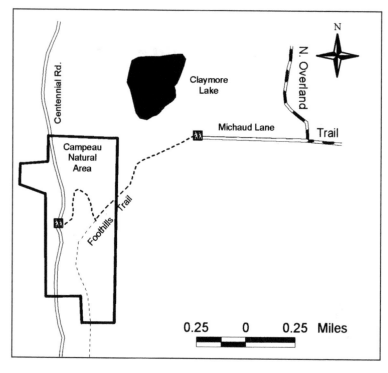

Campeau Natural Area

To Get There

From downtown Fort Collins, take Mulberry Street west to Overland Trail Road, the westernmost road along the city's perimeter. Head north on Overland Trail, following it past Vine Street as it begins to wind. At one of the sharper curves, you'll notice a turning lane leading west (left) down a road that looks to be a straight shot toward the foothills, and a white farmhouse at the corner. The street sign designates the road both as Michaud Lane and CR 50W. Drive west on Michaud Lane 0.5 mile where it dead-ends. You'll find a few parking spots at a closed bridge. This is your trailhead.

The Hike

This short jaunt into the foothills is a nice, easily accessible excursion when you need to shake off those city blues with a bit of open space. The trail leads you into one of the newer natural areas acquired by the city for the preservation of open spaces. The Foothills Trail is an 8-mile connection between the **Campeau Natural Area,** winding along the ridge overlooking Horsetooth Reservoir to the **Maxwell and Pineridge Natural Areas,** all three of which are maintained and patrolled by city employees. (That means, yes, a leash law for dogs is enforced.) Anyone who loves open spaces will be happy to see the city, chunk by chunk, continue piecing together the abundant natural areas that the Fort Collins pioneers found so awe-inspiring.

From the trailhead, cross a rusty iron footbridge and let yourself be conducted down a long corridor between two fences. (The fences are evidence of how difficult it has been for the open-space folks to carve out a natural area in a region that's been privately owned since anyone can remember.) At about 0.75 mile, the fences yawn out onto the yucca and open hillsides. Here the trail veers south (left) and begins its ascent with inspiring views behind you of Claymore Lake glittering between its cottonwoods (the lake falls on private property and is not accessible by this trail).

The trail switchbacks up to a flat shelf where it forks at the 1-mile point. The left fork is a hiker-made trail. The right fork winds up around the back side of a spectacular greenish rock-encrusted cap and onto a windy summit, where a lovely ponderosa pine oasis flourishes. Continue around the bend for grand views of Bellvue Valley and the uptilted slabs of red sandstone that are the northern beginnings of the sandstone hogbacks of Lory State Park a few miles farther south. Round a second bend for views overlooking the sparkling Horsetooth Reservoir and its north dam. From here the trail continues down to a second trailhead off Centennial Road just south of Horsetooth Reservoir's northernmost dam. The Foothills Trail continues another 8 miles, and you can explore a wealth of trail forks made by hikers and deer. This section of the Foothills Trail provides the best get-away-from-it-all feeling, but it is no secret. I visited in early February midweek and encountered multitudes of mountain bikers, joggers, and horseback riders. Keep in mind that rattlesnakes are common in these hills.

Cathy Fromme Prairie Natural Area

▶ **1 mile one way**   ▶ **Easy**

Maps: U.S.G.S. Fort Collins

Beginning Elevation: 5,000 feet

Ending Elevation: 5,100 feet

Access Road: Paved street

Season: Year-round, depending on weather

Connector Trails: Fossil Creek Bike Trail continues in both directions

Highlights: It's worth carting along the binoculars for this superb opportunity to view wildlife and birds across a pristine native short-grass prairie, very accessible on the outskirts of the south side of the city.

To Get There

From downtown Fort Collins, take Mulberry Street to Shields and then Shields Street south past Harmony Road about a mile, where you'll

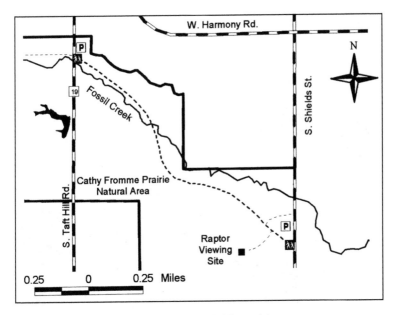

Cathy Fromme Prairie Natural Area

see the parking area and a sign notifying passersby of the trailhead on the right (west). Pull in and park here.

The Hike

This stretch of prairie was named after Cathy Potter Fromme, a city council member who worked for the preservation of open space in the Fort Collins area. At the trailhead, stop and read the informational display that discusses the natural-area designation and the history behind it. This natural area is one of several sections of prairie and foothills property that have been set aside by the city of Fort Collins and Larimer County for public preservation of wild places. The Cathy Fromme Natural Area is a particularly special spot. Because it has never been plowed under, you have a rare opportunity to see nature carving out a balance in the presence of urban progress.

The raptor-viewing station at the Cathy Fromme Natural Area

Before you start walking, continue beyond the fence south a short distance, following signs to the raptor-viewing station. Good interactive displays discuss the intricate relationship between raptors and their prey. The replication of the underground world of the black-tailed prairie dog is particularly fascinating. A great place to bring the kids. And it is certainly possible to catch sight of soaring birds of prey from this spot. On my visit in midwinter, I spotted a bald eagle gliding overhead.

The nature walk itself begins back at the parking lot where you walk down a paved path toward a bicycle underpass, veering left across the prairie. (Fossil Creek Trail continues east under the highway toward several other proposed natural areas on this end of the city.) Continue on the path toward a view of the foothills and **Horsetooth Rock**. A housing development looks out onto the natural area from a ridge above. Along the way, stop to read the various informational displays. Each discusses a different aspect of the short-grass prairie ecosystem and provides clear pictures of the birds and wildlife you might see hunting and romping among the tall grasses. Check out the animal tracks pressed into the cement.

Some birds to watch for are the long-legged mountain plover, the western meadowlark with its yellow belly, ravens, magpies, hawks, eagles, and several varieties of songbirds. Coyotes and badgers also thrive in the prairie landscape. It's interesting to imagine what it might have been like to see buffalo grazing in great herds here or to spy a black bear ambling through. A proposal to reintroduce the endangered black-footed ferret, a critter that helps to keep the prairie dog populations in balance, could be an added delight to visiting this wildlife habitat in the future. Because this area is home to diverse types of wildlife that are easily disrupted by any human presence, remain on the trail, keep your pooch on the trail, and take advantage of binoculars.

After walking the distance across the prairie to a second trailhead located on Taft Hill Road, you can continue under the underpass leading into another chunk of the Cathy Fromme Natural Area to the bottom of the foothills. From here, the Fossil Creek Trail continues on to the

Coyote Ridge Natural Area

▶ 3.75 miles one way   ▶ Moderate

Pineridge Natural Area where it connects with the Foothills Trail.

Maps: U.S.G.S. Loveland

Beginning Elevation: 5,032 feet

Ending Elevation: 5,500 feet

Access Road: Paved road

Season: Year round, depending on weather

Connector Trails: Rimrock Trail; **Blue Sky Trail**

Highlights: Recently expanded trail accessing reclaimed short-grass prairie in the foothills just south of Fort Collins. Offers sensational views of rimrock and a rare plant species found only in this area. Lots of possibilities for further exploration.

To Get There

From downtown Fort Collins, take Mulberry Street to Taft Hill Road and turn left, headed south. From the Taft Hill/Harmony intersection, continue on Taft Hill Road 3.5 miles to the trailhead. You'll know you're close when you see the buck-and-rail fence that borders all city natural areas. The trailhead is well posted on the road in either direction.

The Hike

Although Coyote Ridge is a relatively new natural area, the word has gotten out. On a windy autumn Sunday, I found the parking lot full of horse trailers and vehicles with bike racks. Luckily, the Coyote Ridge Trail

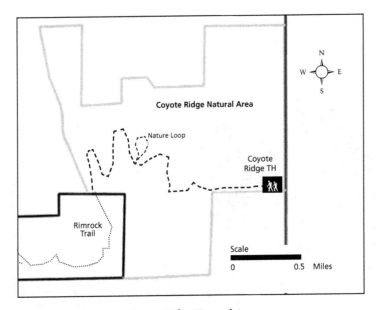

Coyote Ridge Natural Area

accesses a very large checkerboard of open spaces that span from the southern tip of Horsetooth Reservoir all the way to Loveland's **Devil's Backbone**. The Coyote Ridge trailhead is conveniently located halfway between these two destinations and visitors have plenty of elbow room.

Keep in mind that no dogs are allowed in the Coyote Ridge Natural Area. The first section of trail is an interpretive trail with informational displays along the way, following a wide road across the prairie to the foothills. The natural area was established partly as a preservation effort for the rare Bell's twinpod, a small early-flowering yellow plant with silvery leaves that grows only along the Front Range in areas with plenty of shale. The foothills are the uptilted remains of an ancient seafloor, and, interestingly, the layers closest to the plains are the oldest slabs.

The first half of the walk takes you across short-grass prairie that has been reclaimed from over-cultivation. At 1.25 miles, the double track reaches a pit-style restroom and a cabin with a large covered porch with

View from Coyote Gulch

picnic tables. A good place to get out of the sun on a hot summer day when this trail can become scorching. From the rest area, you'll find the main trail heading up into the foothills by following signs visible beyond the bathroom. (Or you can choose to take the interpretive loop counter-clockwise by following a second trail that launches off behind the cabin.) The main trail winds around to find a notch between the rabbitbrush and yucca hillsides, taking you up into a cozy wildflower hollow where deer were grazing on my visit. On another visit, I also encountered a rattlesnake in this picturesque hollow, so watch your feet!

Before switchbacking up to the top of the hill, you'll notice an interpretive display off to your left with a nice view of the plains. At the top of the ridge, your moderately strenuous climb will be rewarded with 360 degree views from colorful lichen cliff tops. It's here, at approximately 2 miles, you may enter the Rimrock Natural Area or choose to conclude your hike. On my visit, I found the temptation to follow the trail down into the valley below hard to resist and the additional 1.25 miles up to the top of the next ridge where the Rimrock Trail intersects the **Blue Sky Trail** well worth the extra effort. Although over every ridge I continually expected to find true open space, the trail never shakes off civilization, homes and ranches (and even a llama farm!) close by the entire route, a reminder of the kind of careful diplomacy it must have taken to bring this open space into the public's hands.

From the **Blue Sky Trail** intersection at 3.75 miles, vistas of grand sandstone cliffs offer opportunities to see raptors circling. A cottonwood grove below might make a cool destination for those seeking a longer adventure. It's possible to make a return trip by way of a small loop which links back to the main trail, returning you to your car.

25 Environmental Learning Center

▶ **1 mile one way**   ▶ **Easy**

Maps: U.S.G.S Fort Collins

Beginning Elevation: 4,875 feet

Ending Elevation: 4,891 feet

Access Road: Last 0.25 mile good gravel road, all cars

Season: Year-round, depending on weather

Connector Trails: Cache la Poudre bike path continues in both directions.

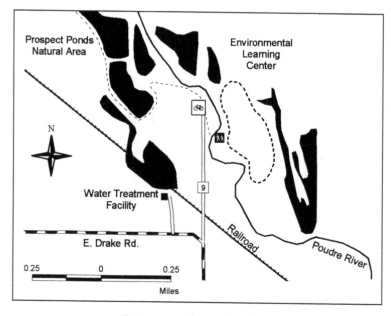

Environmental Learning Center

Highlights: A raptor center, cottonwoods, fascinating history, a
secluded riparian area with many opportunities for wildlife
viewing. A true natural area in the very shadow of the city.

To Get There

The access to this trailhead is a bit tricky. Take Drake Road east past
Timberline Drive until it crosses through some cornfields and passes
the water treatment plant. Continue just beyond the treatment plant
driveway, crossing a narrow bridge at a bend in the road and turning
left onto a dirt road with a sign "Environmental Learning Center" sitting
inconspicuously to one side. Drive about 0.25 mile on the dirt road to
its dead end at a parking area. Note the little white house as you drive
in; it was built in 1870 by Jesse and Frederick Sherwood, the first white
settlers along this stretch of the Poudre River.

Cottonwoods along the Cache la Poudre River

The Hike

Before starting your walk, proceed beyond the picnic area to a clapboard-fronted building sitting back from a picnic area. This is the Raptor Center where injured birds of prey, unable to survive in the wild, live in captivity but serve an educational purpose. These birds include golden eagles, bald eagles, red-tailed hawks, great horned owls, and turkey vultures, and many of them were injured while feeding along highways. Their naturally dominant personalities make them less likely to fly away (as crows or magpies do) at the sign of an approaching vehicle. Take your time quietly observing these majestic creatures.

There are two trail options from here. One is to take the paved bicycle path from the parking area as the trail parallels the Poudre River, a buck-and-rail fence lining the way. Just out of sight across the river are several ponds set aside for bird habitat. Some birds to watch for are

Canada geese, mallards, kingfishers, ospreys, and great blue herons. The bike path continues over a footbridge and through multiple natural areas, crossing Prospect Road and eventually meeting up with the **Lee Martinez** section of the Poudre bike trail; almost the entire stretch is in natural settings with the Poudre River always nearby. This section of bike path is truly a Fort Collins treasure.

The second walk is restricted to foot traffic only, and pets are prohibited due to the delicacy of the wildlife habitat. (If you've brought the dog, the bike path is a good choice with plenty of romping space.) The trailhead is just up the paved path from the parking area where a soft path takes off, crossing a swaying footbridge over the river. The path loops around on an interpretive trail (obtain leaflets from the visitor center) through a tangled stand of cottonwoods, a beautiful spot in autumn. Watch for muskrats swimming in the calmer waters of the Cache la Poudre River and deer grazing in the grassy meadows at dawn and dusk. It's strange to find such a healthy natural space so close to zooming traffic, visible and audible from most of the trail.

An interesting note is that the area now designated as the Environmental Learning Center was once used by the Arapaho as a village campsite. The Arapaho were friendly with the white settlers, and their hospitable nature explains why Fort Collins was never much of a fort, lacking defensive walls or any sort of stockade. Frederick Sherwood, who settled this spot, was appointed an Indian agent in 1864 and provided Chief Friday's Arapaho band refuge while Friday unsuccessfully attempted to arrange a reservation on the Poudre River. Chief Friday, who attended white schools and had been adopted at childhood by the famous trapper Thomas Fitzpatrick, eventually arranged to share the Wind River Reservation with the Shoshones in Wyoming. (See the introduction for more history about Chief Friday.)

Fossil Creek Reservoir

▶ 0.25 to 2.25 miles one way ▶ Easy

Maps: Loveland

Beginning Elevation: 4,900

Ending Elevation: 4,870

Access Road: Paved road

Distance: **Heron Loop:** 0.25 miles
Sandpiper Trail: 1 mile round trip
Cattails Flats Loop: 2.25 miles

Season: Summer and fall (closed during winter and spring)

Connector Trails: None

Highlights: Birder's paradise! Viewing blinds provide great opportunities to watch Colorado's plethora of bird species on a reservoir located in a restored shortgrass prairie.

To Get There

Take College Avenue south past Harmony Street 3 miles. Continue past the flea markets on your left, then past Trilby Road, to Carpenter Road (CR32). Go east on Carpenter Road a distance of 4 miles. You'll notice the county open space's buck and rail fence on your left as you near Timberline Road, but this section of the Fossil Creek Open Space is closed to visitors. Continue past Timberline to the entrance, a green gate on your left with a dark brown Fossil Creek Reservoir sign. The gate is locked at sunset and only daytime visits are allowed. Drive down the paved road to the parking area where you'll see several displays and a

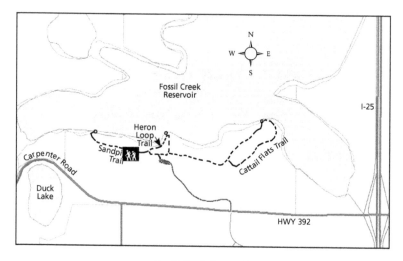

Fossil Creek Reservoir

large new bathroom with lots of windows. Entrance to the area is by donation.

The Hike

Before heading out, stop and read the dry eraser display board near the restroom where avid students of ornithology have recorded the month's sightings. At my visit during the fall migrations, people recorded sightings of avocets, golden eyes, peregrine falcons, egrets and many, many more. All this within earshot of I-80! This display also gives you a good idea what to look for since 180 different species have been spotted at this reservoir making identification a tricky business.

Keep in mind that Fossil Creek Reservoir is seasonally closed to visitors to give the wildlife a break during the spring and winter months when their resources are most strained and when they're nesting. Dogs, bikes and horses are not allowed at the reservoir.

There are three trails launching off from the trailhead and depending on the water level you may decide to do all or only one or two of them. During my visit in late September, the water level was too low to view many birds on the Sandpiper Trail located at the west end of the reservoir. (The north side of the reservoir is a wildlife refuge closed to visitors.)

Sandpiper Trail: The Heron Loop is a short, paved, wheelchair-accessible path that takes you down to some sheltered picnic spots and to a great viewing platform where I found the best vantage to watch birds in late autumn when the water level was quite low. The Sandpiper Trail takes off from the far west side of the Heron Loop and turns to improved gravel. During my visit, construction was underway on a swath of land intersecting the trail. The viewing blind is located amongst the cottonwoods 0.5 mile from the trailhead. Colorful displays can be found inside the blinds identifying many of the birds you might see, and when. After spending some time bird watching, return the way you came. From here you can make your way across the Heron Loop to the Cattails Loop to visit the second blind.

Cattail Flats Loop: This longer loop starts on the east side of the Heron Loop and is clearly marked. Follow the improved gravel trail up over the gentle slope of a recently restored shortgrass prairie. In the future, we're sure to see more and more wildlife flocking to the area as the prairie matures. In the meantime, this section of trail can feel exposed to sun and wind, traversing the hillside at a great a distance from the water's edge where you'd rather be exploring. Be patient and you'll be amply rewarded when you reach the blind and find the bird's undisturbed.

Fossil Creek flows through the Fort Collins sanitation facility upstream to empty into the reservoir where the water serves as a holding tank for irrigation water for the area's farmers. (To learn more about the reservoir's function in the county's water system, see a display near the trailhead.) It's through the cooperation of several community entities that the reservoir has been livable for waterfowl and wildlife. Even during my not-so-well timed trip at mid-afternoon (the best time to watch birds is early morning or evening), I still observed several great blue herons, red-necked grebes, American coots, American white pelicans, Canadian geese, gulls, terns, and meadowlarks.

When you're done at the blind, follow the loop along a grove of cottonwoods and out across the prairie for more bird watching possibilities. You'll notice a nesting stand where hawks or osprey might make their home in the summer months. Be sure to stop at a display near the top of the loop where a diagram allows you to identify the names of the mountains on a clear day. Views of the Front Range are unbeatable on the last leg of this loop.

 Lee Martinez Park

▶ **2 miles round trip**   ▶ **Easy**

Maps: U.S.G.S. Fort Collins

Beginning Elevation: 4,980 feet

Ending Elevation: 4,985 feet

Access Road: Paved street

Season: Year-round, depending on weather

Connector Trails: Some sections of the loop are part of the Fort Collins bike trail system and continue in both directions.

Highlights: Urban trail along the Poudre River in one of the city's most beloved and historic natural areas. Good opportunities for wildlife viewing and further explorations.

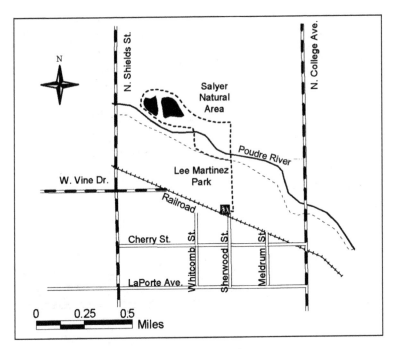

Lee Martinez Park

To Get There

Take College Avenue north past Laporte Avenue, turning left onto Cherry Street and then right onto Sherwood Street. (There is a sign for Lee Martinez Park at the intersection.) Follow Sherwood Street north over the railroad tracks and into the park. The parking area is between the softball diamonds and the tennis courts. You will see a paved bike path taking off from the north end of the parking lot. This is your trailhead.

The Hike

Lee Martinez Park was named after an outspoken and visionary citizen who served on the Fort Collins Human Relations Commission in the 1930s and 1940s, working to abolish "White Trade Only" signs that

A side path at Lee Martinez Park

began to spring up around town and to combat other racial problems. Lee Martinez moved to Fort Collins at the age of 17. Like many immigrants from Spain of the era, he worked in the sugar beet fields along with his father, who was field boss and interpreter. Lee Martinez Park commemorates the Spanish Americans who went to work every day in beet fields very near where the park now sits.

To begin, walk north toward the line of cottonwood trees camouflaging the river. You will immediately encounter several trails headed in all four directions. At the map display, go right (east) on a path marked "Hickory Street Trail." Follow it as it curves around to a large metal footbridge that spans the Poudre River at a shady spot under the mammoth old cottonwoods. The trail continues across the Salyer Natural Area to intersect a dirt road. The paved bike path continues straight, but to continue the loop walk, turn left on the dirt road, headed west. At the end of this dirt road, it curves into a small fenced parking area with a dirt path leading out toward a lake beyond. This small lake is a nice spot to do some bird watching on a quiet summer morning, and a soft path provides access to pockets of wetlands where a great assortment of birds thrive year-round. Lee Martinez Park, with its mix of meadows, riverlands, wetlands, and urban proximity, gives many wild animals a place to call home. Loop around the lake on a narrow, unofficial foot path. After completing the loop, pick up another small track that leaves the lake to follow the bank of the river through a dense thicket of underbrush and cottonwoods to a concrete footbridge that reconnects you to the paved Lee Martinez bike trail. Take a left here, heading back on the last leg of the loop east, returning to your vehicle the way you came.

If you have children (or even if you don't), I recommend a stop at the petting farm, visible on the other side of the park as brightly painted red barns and a grain silo. This historic farm was built in 1920 by J. P. Nelson and restored by Fort Collins Parks and Recreation in 1985.

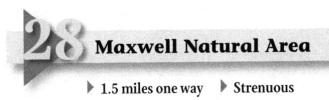

28 Maxwell Natural Area

▶ **1.5 miles one way** ▶ **Strenuous**

Maps: U.S.G.S. Horsetooth Reservoir
Beginning Elevation: 5,200 feet
Ending Elevation: 5,640 feet
Access Road: Paved street
Season: Year-round, depending on weather

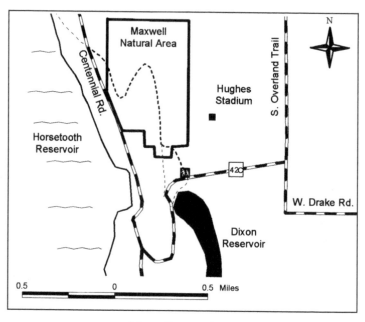

Maxwell Natural Area

Connector Trails: This trail is part of the 8-mile Foothills Trail, connecting with both the Pineridge and the **Campeau Natural Area Trails.**

Highlights: Fascinating ascent through interesting rocks and plant life, passing just below the notorious "A" (painted on the side of the foothills by Colorado State University [CSU] students) for views of the city and Horsetooth Reservoir.

To Get There

From downtown Fort Collins, take Mulberry Street all the way west to Overland Trail Road and turn left (south). Continue on Overland Trail past Prospect Street and Hughes Stadium, turning right (west) on the first road (posted CR 42C) south of the stadium grounds. The turnoff is across the road from the Holiday Twin drive-in theater and is one of the access roads to Horsetooth Reservoir. Just before CR 42C bends and curves up the hill at the bottom of the dam, turn right into a gravel parking area.

Find the trailhead just before a "Trail Crossing" road sign on the right. (The **Pineridge Trail** continues from Dixon Reservoir.) Walk between two boulders and down a corridor between two teetering fence lines.

The Hike

The trail begins by crossing behind CSU's Hughes Stadium through a wide swath of grassland with views above of the painted "A". Follow the path as it veers left (west) along a buck-and-rail fence. The trail crosses a gravel road where a sign "City of Fort Collins" is visible on the ridge above. Hike toward this sign, crossing a (usually) dry ditch to reach it. The sign marks the boundary of the Maxwell Natural Area. From the sign, the trail is easy to follow along the foot of the hillside, crossing a footbridge and meeting with a scattering of robust ponderosa pines where the path clearly forks. If you miss the fork, you'll know it, because you'll soon cross two more footbridges. (If you miss the first side trail, you can pick up another soon after the two footbridges.) The lower trail continues north to serve two purposes: It connects with the Foothills Trail where it climbs around a fenced concrete pad and stays high on the hillside. It also curves around on a jogger's loop back toward the stadium.

The hike I propose here takes the nature enthusiast up a series of switchbacks through rocky, lichen-covered terrain. The climb is short and steep, traversing chest-high mountain mahogany brush and stands of velvet-leafed mullein. If you are interested in visiting the "A" up close, watch through the brush for sight of the white-washed rocks and find a foot path leading you through the dense branches to reach it. (While you're there, pack out any paint buckets or other litter you might find left behind.) If you visit during warmer months, be aware that rattlesnakes do thrive on rocky hillsides. Once you reach the crest of the hill, follow the path across grassy meadows where deer sometimes graze at dawn and dusk. Interesting stunted ponderosas grow out of the hillside, defying the high winds that can often whistle through this gap in the hogbacks. From here, enjoy satisfying views of the city and plains. Centennial Road and Horsetooth Reservoir can be accessed on the other side of the meadow to the west.

 Pineridge Natural Area

▶ **2 miles one way**   ▶ **Easy**

Maps: U.S.G.S. Horsetooth Reservoir

Beginning Elevation: 5,200 feet

Ending Elevation: 5,400 feet

Access Road: Paved county road

Season: Year-round, depending on weather

Connector Trails: The Pineridge Trail described here is part of the 8-mile Foothills Trail and accesses the **Maxwell** and **Campeau Natural Areas.**

Highlights: A stately cottonwood grove, a lake, ponderosa pine foothills—all within the city limits!

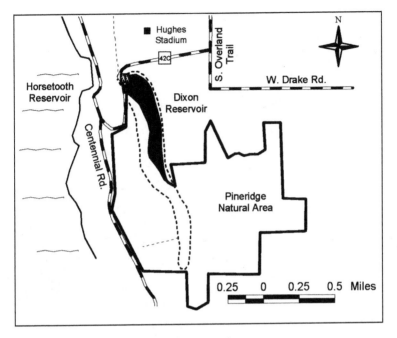

Pineridge Natural Area

To Get There

The directions to the trailhead for this walk are the same as those described in this book for the **Maxwell Natural Area** walk. From downtown Fort Collins, take Mulberry Street west to Overland Trail Road and turn left, heading south. Continue on Overland Trail past Prospect Street and Hughes Stadium, turning right (west) onto the first road south of the stadium grounds (posted CR 42C). The turnoff is across the road from the Holiday Twin drive-in theater. Just before CR 42C makes a sharp bend at the bottom of the dam, turn right into a gravel parking area.

To find the trailhead, walk up the road toward the dam past the "Trail Crossing" sign. Past the private-property boundary are two well-beaten paths leading down into a dense thicket of cottonwoods.

The cottonwood grove at Pineridge Natural Area

The Hike

It's possible to start this walk from the parking lot at Dixon Reservoir, but that means missing out on this unique ramble through the lush understory of a cottonwood grove.

The trail soon comes out onto the shores of Dixon Reservoir, bypassing the parking area above. On the day I visited, a drizzly spring day, I observed many waterfowl on the lake, including several great blue herons huddling perturbed against the unseasonable weather. Herons often nest in cottonwood groves.

As you continue past the lake, crossing a footbridge near the Dixon Reservoir parking area, stay on the high trail. This narrow path leads along the tree line dividing the prairie from the foothills ecosystem where stunted ponderosa pines and mountain mahogany grow. The directions given here take the nature lover on a tour of the more wilderness-oriented walk in the Pineridge Natural Area. Much of the preserve is zigzagged with wide, dusty mountain bike trails, and if you're on foot, you might think you've stumbled onto a rally course for dirt bikes. The high trail is a treasure, offering a bit of riparian elements, a lot of prairie, and a healthy dose of foothills blended together nicely in one short stroll.

The trail continues to the 2-mile point where it encounters an access road to Horsetooth Reservoir, CR 38E. (However, the trail can't be accessed from here, as it is buffered by private property.) You can explore a number of hiker-made side trails branching up into the forest. The best of these can be found near the end of the trail, climbing along a sheer red cliff to the top of Spring Canyon Dam for views of Horsetooth Reservoir, the city, and the surrounding area.

To return, either retrace your steps, or drop onto the lower trail along the prairie floor to make a loop of the hike. Either way, I recommend walking back via the opposite east shore of Dixon Reservoir where a variety of deciduous trees grow, providing a perfect blind to observe the bird life. After you cross the small dam and revisit the cottonwood grove, return to your vehicle the way you came.

POUDRE CANYON
AREA TRAILS

PINGREE PARK

Located 25 miles up the Poudre Canyon, the road into Pingree Park follows the South Fork of the Cache la Poudre River as it carves its long and wild course down from its source off Rowe Peak in Rocky Mountain National Park. Pingree Park was set aside by Congress as public land in 1912 with 1,600 acres for the use of the Colorado A&M College, the predecessor of Colorado State University (CSU). Currently, CSU owns much of Pingree Valley, and the facilities there are used for university natural studies programs, elder hostels, and an environmental educational camp for sixth graders.

However, the area surrounding the campus is managed by Roosevelt National Park. Many of the trails from Pingree Park access the Comanche Peak Wilderness, closed to all mechanized modes of travel, or Rocky Mountain National Park, which does not allow dogs and requires a backcountry permit for overnight camping. No permit is required for day hikes.

Pingree Park is named after George Pingree, one of the first pioneers to settle in the area and a character straight out of the old Wild West mold. He was a soldier under Colonel John Chivington's Third Regiment at Sand Creek. He liked to show off where he'd taken an arrow through the cheek and lost some teeth. At the Sand Creek massacre, he took many scalps from the Arapaho and Cheyenne and was known to exchange them for free haircuts at a barbershop in Denver. However, most of the peaks and place-names of Pingree Park derive from the Koenig family, whose old homestead cabins can still be seen on the CSU Pingree Park campus by walking the **Pingree Valley Loop Trail. Emmaline Lake** was named after Frank Koenig's mother, and Frank's wife named Ypsilon Mountain when she noticed that its permanent snowfield formed the shape of the letter Y.

Browns Lake Trail #941

▸ **4.5 miles one way**   ▸ **Moderate**

Maps: U.S.G.S. Kinikinik, Comanche Peak

Beginning Elevation: 10,400 feet

Ending Elevation: 10,600 feet

Access Road: Good gravel road last 15 miles

Season: Midsummer to fall

Connector Trails: Old Flowers Trail, Comanche Reservoir Trail

Highlights: Alpine hike past a rocky summit to some high, fishable cirque lakes tucked into a dramatic basin with wildflowers and views.

To Get There

From Ted's Place (junction of 287 and 14), take Highway 14 up the Poudre Canyon 25 miles to the Pingree Park turnoff, just past Kelly Flats.

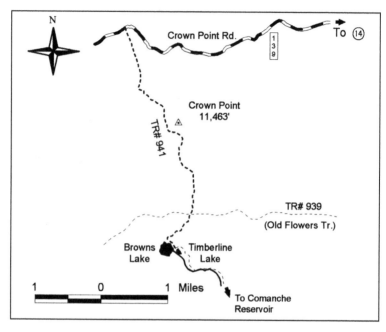

Browns Lake Trail #941

If you reach Eggers fishing access, you've gone too far. Stay on Pingree Park Road 63E and go 4 miles to the Crown Point Road fork. A sign at the intersection points to Browns Lake. Take a right and continue on this road (FR 139) 11 miles farther to the Browns Lake trailhead. Parking is plentiful, but there are no restrooms.

The Hike

Be sure to get an extra early start for this hike. Much of its distance takes you above timberline, and afternoon thunderstorms and lightning strikes are a very real threat.

No camping is allowed at the trailhead, but you can find a few nice spots along Crown Point Road. The trailhead is located across the road from the parking lot at a gap in the buck-and-rail fence. The trail begins

Browns Lake

to climb steadily through the rocky, exposed terrain where limber pines thrive and the black-and-white-feathered Clark's Nutcrackers scurry to collect their nuts. The views open onto the craggy ridge leading up to Crown Point to the east (the point itself is obscured until the pass) with the Mummy Range to the west. Don't let the elevations I've listed here fool you. Crown Point rises to 11,463 feet, and you must climb the saddle just a few hundred feet below. Crown Point is one of two high ridges you must mount before descending to the lakes. The Comanche Peak Wilderness boundary is crossed at the Crown Point pass at the 2-mile point. The views of the Mummies from this spot are dizzying. Be sure to carry plenty of water; because most of the hike is done well above timberline, the thin air at such altitudes can be dehydrating.

Once inside the wilderness boundary, the trail drops down into a grassy valley before climbing a second ridge, all the time traversing alpine tundra fringed by "krummholz," subalpine firs stunted by the extreme climate. After dropping off this second ridge, the path enters some lovely forest and bisects the Old Flowers Trail at 3.25 miles, a historic road built by a man named Flowers to access the mining town of **Lulu City** from Fort Collins. An old cabin marks the trail crossing.

Vistas of the massive precipice above Browns Lake are visible as you descend into the basin. The wildflowers along this stretch of trail are often abuzz midsummer with bumblebees busily pollinating the arnica, lupine, bistort, asters, and paintbrush that grow here. Nine numbered and designated campsites can be found along the trail past the Flowers Trail junction.

Three lakes (the smallest, no more than a glorified pond, is unnamed) lie deep green beneath the dark furrowed brow of the dramatic cliff face. Fishing in Timberline Lake, the southernmost lake, is good, yielding brookies grown chubby on alpine insect life.

It is possible to make a two-car shuttle of the hike by parking a second vehicle at Comanche Reservoir at the end of FR 145, adding 2.5 miles to your one-way mileage.

Emmaline Lake Trail #954

▶ **6.5 miles one way** ▶ **Strenuous**

Maps: U.S.G.S. Comanche Peak

Beginning Elevation: 8,960 feet

Ending Elevation: 11,000 feet

Access Road: Good gravel road last 15.5 miles

Season: Midsummer to fall

Connector Trails: Mummy Pass Trail

Highlights: Cirque meadows, lush old-growth forest, and two high-country lakes make this one of the most popular of the Pingree Park trails.

To Get There

From Ted's Place (junction of 287 and 14), take Highway 14 up Poudre Canyon 25 miles to the Pingree Park turnoff where you cross a large metal bridge. The turnoff is located between Kelly Flats and Eggers. Take the Pingree Park Road 14.5 miles to the turnoff to Tom Bennett Campground (FR 145) and turn left. Continue 0.5 mile past the campground to the Cirque Meadows trailhead. Parking is limited, although 4WD vehicles can access more parking on a rough road that continues in beyond the trailhead.

The Hike

From the trailhead, walk the rough 4WD road a distance of 0.5 mile. This road is open to motorized travel up to a road closure at a green gate

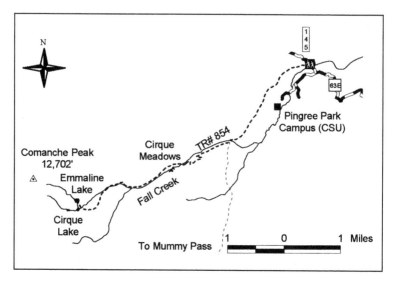

Emmaline Lake Trail #954

and can be used for overflow parking, although there's not much space and a high-clearance vehicle is recommended. At the gate, where foot travel only begins, the path enters forest claimed by the July 1, 1994, Hourglass fire, the result of a lightning strike. Aspens already grow head-high, and wildflowers flourish, giving the area a fresh feeling of renewal unique to forests after fire.

By mile 2, the trail has approached the roar of a waterfall and soon after traverses two log footbridges overlooking the cascades. A campsite can be found at the trail junction where the Mummy Pass Trail forks off. The trail continues to climb at a leisurely pace through mixed forest, the creek tumbling just out of view. I have designated this trail strenuous due to the difficulty of the last leg; but the hike into the Cirque Meadows, a distance of 3 miles, is easy.

From the Cirque Meadows, views of the Mummy Range are magical. There are more designated campsites around the perimeter of the

Views of the Mummy Range from the Cirque Meadows

meadow and along a logging road to the left. At the Cirque Meadows, be sure to go right over a footbridge beyond a trail sign. Beyond here, no horses are allowed, and dogs inside the Comanche Peak Wilderness must be leashed.

The upper stretches of the Emmaline Trail encounter forest that exudes an ancient feel, very hushed and sun-dappled with many easy creek crossings over log footbridges. The path narrows, and you will climb more strenuously toward your destination, criss-crossing past multiple small and large waterfalls. One particularly spectacular waterfall reminds me of the Minneconjou, a band of the Sioux named after waterfalls where they believed the presence of the Creator could be felt most strongly.

The last 2-mile leg of the trail into the Emmaline Lake basin proceeds through boulder fields, and sometimes you must follow rock cairns. There are designated campsites along the way, although no camping is allowed within about 1.5 miles of the lake. Just above a wide waterfall, you reach the smaller lake below Emmaline. Emmaline Lake is a few hundred yards above. Lined on all sides by pink cliffs, the lakes drain the east side of Comanche Peak (invisible from this vantage). The mountain is so massive that it requires two basins to drain it; **Mirror Lake** drains it to the west. Emmaline Lake has recently suffered winter-kill and has not been restocked for fishing. That doesn't detract from the loveliness of Emmaline Lake, though, with its many small coves and views of the soaring basin walls above.

Fish Creek Trail #1009

▶ **5 miles one way** ▶ **Moderate**

Maps: U.S.G.S. Pingree Park

Beginning Elevation: 9,080 feet

Ending Elevation: 7,960 feet

Access Road: Medium-grade gravel road last 2 miles

Season: Early summer to fall

Connector Trails: Beaver Creek Trail and Little Beaver Creek Trail

Highlights: Superb views of Pingree Park area on the drive in, rewarding the trekker with a creek-side hike of great natural diversity: views, meadows, geology, wildflowers—this place has it all. Especially suited to a two-car shuttle.

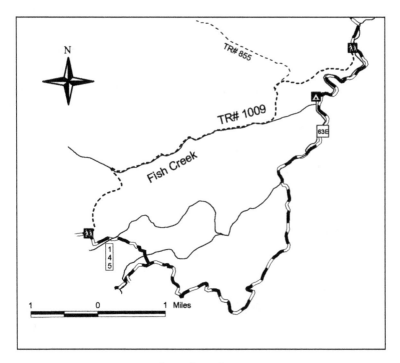

Fish Creek Trail #1009

To Get There

From Ted's Place (junction of 287 and 14), take Highway 14 up the Poudre Canyon 25 miles to the Pingree Park turnoff, located between Kelly Flats Campground and Eggers fishing access. Cross the bridge and continue 8 miles to the Fish Creek trailhead, trying to keep your eyes on the road and off the beautiful views of the canyon below. If you do the two-car shuttle, leave one car at the Fish Creek trailhead and continue another 8 miles to the Beaver Creek trailhead turnoff (before the Pingree Park campus). This road, FR 145, is well marked but a bit rough. Drive past the Tom Bennett campground another 1.5 miles to the trailhead at Sky Ranch, where you can park your second car and begin hiking along the Fish Creek Trail to the first car waiting below.

The Hike

Two trails depart from the Beaver Creek trailhead: the Beaver Creek Trail to **Browns Lake** and the Fish Creek Trail to the Fish Creek trailhead. The Fish Creek Trail begins as an old logging road through lodgepole pine and subalpine firs, then veers north (left) near the top of the hill. After the trail dips out of the pines, it soon begins to wind through a quiet lush area of mixed aspen and fir. Glimpses of a small, willowy meadow may offer wildlife-viewing possibilities. At the spot where the path fords the burbling Fish Creek, a special feeling hovers over the place. This little microcosm is a still, serene place to sit and listen to the water flow past on its way from the snowfields where it melted to the Poudre River somewhere downstream.

Just after the creek crossing, the path changes direction, swerving northeast down the canyon. The path leads the trekker on a soul-soothing meander through a well-jumbled mix of pine, aspen, fir, spruce, and, on the lower half of the trail, handsome ponderosa pines, with Fish Creek always rushing alongside. At times the trail plunges into lush, dense stands of deep, dark firs, only to emerge on the side of the rocky canyon wall with views across wildflower meadows of the gorge below.

At about midway along the trail, an aspen-encircled park is a great destination if you want only a short stroll from either trailhead.

As you cross a wide-open meadow bordered by twisted, lightning-struck ponderosas and rock formations, the trail becomes overgrown, and you may have to follow cairns (rock piles). From this grassy knoll, take in the fantastic vistas of White Rock Mountain across the South Fork of the Poudre River to the northeast. Only later can you make out signs of the quarry still in use on this landmark. At the trail junction with the Little Beaver Creek Trail, continue straight. You will face some moderately strenuous climbing as the trail swerves away from the creek, ascending the canyon wall to tread through the drier, rockier country favored by ponderosa pine. Overall, Fish Creek Trail provides excellent

Views of the South Fork of the Poudre River from the Fish Creek Trail

opportunities to see a little of every sort of northern Colorado life zone.

If you do the hike from Fish Creek up to the Beaver Creek trailhead at Sky Ranch, it could be somewhat more strenuous, especially at the start where the trail zigzags up the canyon wall.

Stormy Peaks Trail #980

▶ **6 miles one way**   ▶ **Moderate**

Maps: U.S.G.S. Pingree Park

Beginning Elevation: 9,000 feet

Ending Elevation: 12,148 feet

Access Road: Good gravel road last 15 miles

Season: Midsummer to fall

Connector Trails: Denny's Point, Twin Lakes Trail, and Rocky Mountain National Park access.

Highlights: Cool, moist forest walk with grand views of Pingree Valley to the summit of a peak in Rocky Mountain National Park.

To Get There

From Ted's Place at the junction of 287 and 14, take Highway 14 up Poudre Canyon 25 miles to the Pingree Park turnoff that crosses a large metal bridge. The turnoff is just west of Kelly Flats. If you reach Eggers fishing access, you've gone too far. Stay on Pingree Park Road 63E 15 miles past the turnoff to CSU's Pingree Park campus to where the road dead-ends at the trailhead parking area.

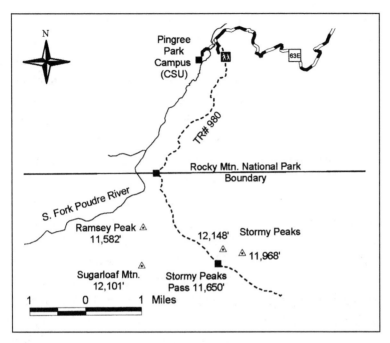

Stormy Peaks Trail #980

The Hike

From the trailhead, walk along the trail as it proceeds through a regenerating wildfire burn. Already, after only a few years, the aspens and wildflowers have moved in. The July 1, 1994, Hourglass fire was the result of a lightning strike.

At 0.75 mile, the trail meets the Denny's Point Trail and at 1 mile encounters the Twin Lakes Trail. The path climbs moderately along a parallel route to the Pingree Valley below, reaching the Comanche Peak Wilderness boundary at 2.5 miles. Soon after entering the wilderness area, you'll find a superb overlook from a sheer precipice onto the valley below and the ponds and lakes of its upper reaches. The trail then swerves into lush north-facing slopes that permeate the senses with the smells and sounds of trickling springs; these run even in periods of severe drought.

At 3.75 miles, the trail crosses into Rocky Mountain National Park. Keep in mind that no dogs are allowed in the park. Be sure to obtain a backcountry permit if you plan to camp overnight within the park's boundaries. As you climb toward timberline, you will be able to see Ramsey Peak (11,582 feet) and Sugarloaf Peak (12,101 feet) farther south across a dark gorge to the west. To the east, the long ridge of false peaks leads up to Stormy Peaks. A good campsite is available just before the trail ascends into alpine tundra. To reach Stormy Peaks Pass, continue along the foot of the ridge to the 6-mile point. Stormy Peaks are easily summited from the pass, although deciding which of several false peaks is the highest can be difficult. The highest point is the westernmost peak and is visible from the pass. Sugarloaf Peak can also be summited from Stormy Peaks Pass. The trail continues over the pass on a network of park trails to Lost Lake.

A warning: Stormy Peaks were named as a reminder of their propensity for severe weather. Sudden afternoon thunderstorms descend out of nowhere. To guarantee your safety, start your hike as early as possible, and plan to be off the mountain by early afternoon. Plan on about six hours round-trip. During my visit to the area, I was on the trail by 8 a.m. and at the foot of the mountain by 11 a.m., but dark circling clouds were a sign not to attempt the last leg to the summit. Moral of the story: Always be willing to turn back.

LOWER POUDRE CANYON

Some of the most well-known northern Colorado hiking can be found along the lower stretches of the Cache la Poudre River. The most famous hike is the **Greyrock Summit Trail,** and the hype is well-deserved. The lower elevations (below 8,000 feet) of the Poudre Canyon flourish in ponderosa pine and Douglas fir and usually provide year-round hiking opportunities (unless it's a particularly snowy winter, in which case many of these trails are splendid snowshoeing destinations). The Poudre River, engorged with melted runoff from its many tributaries, has been designated a Wild and Scenic River, the only one in the state of Colorado. Much of the hiking in the lower Poudre Canyon takes the trekker up along gulches and creek draws of great lushness and diversity. Some trails are open to mechanized travel such as bikes and all-terrain vehicles (ATVs). However, **Mount McConnel** lies inside the Cache la Poudre Wilderness and is therefore closed to all but foot travel. Roosevelt National Forest requires dogs to be leashed.

The Cache la Poudre River was named for the time the founding father of Larimer County, Antoine Janis, only a young lad, accompanied his trapper father and some other French trappers on a trip up the river. When their wagon broke down, they were forced to unload some of the heavier items and cache them along the river to return for later; the major item hidden was a supply of gunpowder. Later, Janis reported that he had stashed the powder, but other sources show that he was only a boy at the time. A plaque has been placed in the spot where the powder was cached in the town of Bellvue, outside Fort Collins.

Dadd Gulch

▶ 3.75 miles one way ▶ Moderate

Maps: U.S.G.S. Rustic

Beginning Elevation: 7,000 feet

Ending Elevation: 8,240 feet

Access Road: Paved highway

Season: Year-round, depending on weather

Connector Trails: Salt Cabin Park 4WD road

Highlights: A creek-side ramble through aspen, narrowleaf cottonwood, and ponderosa pine forest with views of Poudre Canyon and some interesting rocks to boot.

To Get There

From Ted's Place (junction of 287 and 14), take Highway 14 up the Poudre Canyon 27.5 miles to Indian Meadows, where you'll find the trailhead near the west end between the resort and the picnic area, both a short distance east of the town of Rustic. The open views of the canyon from the Dadd Gulch trailhead at Indian Meadows are among the loveliest in all of Poudre Canyon.

The Hike

Walk beyond the sign past a corral, through two gates, swinging right up the gorge into the cool shade of the narrowleaf cottonwoods that grow in healthy abundance along Dadd Creek. Also expect to find plenty of ponderosas, junipers, aspens, and Douglas firs at this

Dadd Gulch

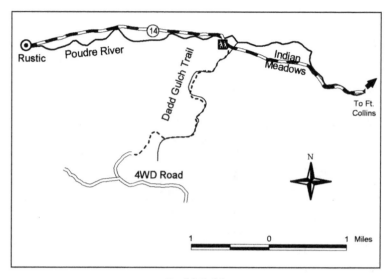

Dadd Gulch

elevation. As the trail crosses and recrosses Dadd Creek, the water's soothing sound matches the close, secluded feeling of trekking up a small gulch such as this one. Every gulch in the canyon is unique. Before venturing to higher altitudes, the trail strays along the rocky walls of the canyon, and you wade through hip-high grasses in the fall, wildflower meadows in summer. At this point, the trail meets up with some utility lines, and you walk along directly beneath them for the better part of a quarter mile before the trail takes one side of the creek and the wires the other. At a crook in the canyon, the path climbs momentarily into drier ponderosa country, the perfect place to spy the blue Steller's jay and the tufty-eared Abert's squirrel. Soon after, you reemerge into the depths of some of the lushest creek-side habitat to be found in the Poudre Canyon country. Come during early summer to find the area blooming with wild primrose.

At 2.25 miles, the trail leaves the creek behind. The red granite rock formations loom straight up from trailside as the climb grows more strenuous. Pass through widely spaced forest (typical of a ponderosa forest at its healthiest) and continue on the trail toward the top of the gulch. You'll pass a spring piped out into an overflowing metal trough, a good place to water the horse if you're on horseback but unreliable for human consumption. Soon after this landmark, you reach a flat spot with a distinctly more alpine feel (subalpine firs and Engelmann spruce among the pines). From here the trail becomes a 4WD road, but it also is a rewarding destination to stand atop a rock and take in the views of Poudre Canyon and, to the south, Salt Creek Park. As an alternate route, the 4WD road can be reached by way of Crown Point Road during summer months when its gate is open. Due to the thick tree coverage, views of Dadd Gulch itself are limited. The gulch was named for an elderly black pioneer everyone called Dad, who lived in a cabin he'd built along the creek, later named Dadd Creek, in the 1880s. The reason for the change in spelling goes unrecorded.

This trail is a favorite with mountain bikers and, due to its accessibility to Highway 14, does not provide much solitude except toward the top of the trail. I recommend hiking Dadd Gulch in the autumn for changing colors or any evening for the fascinating light on the rocks.

35 Gateway Mountain Park

▶ 0.75 mile one way   ▶ Difficult

Maps: Laporte
Beginning Elevation: 5,374 feet
Ending Elevation: 6,164 feet

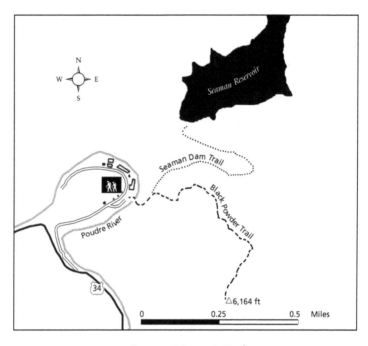

Gateway Mountain Park

Access Road: Good gravel road, last 0.5 mile

Season: Year round, depending on weather

Connector Trails: Trail continues along river to Seaman Reservoir

Highlights: Short but lovely trail through ponderosas to a ridge
overlooking Poudre Canyon

To Get There

From Ted's Place (junction of Highways 287 and 14), take Highway
14 up the canyon 5.5 miles. At this point, you'll come to the top of the hill
where a sign is visible on the right marked "Gateway Mountain Park."
Take a right at this turn-off down through a steep narrow niche in the
rocks to a parking/picnic area. Stop and pay your $4 entrance fee, then

Poudre River at Gateway Mountain Park

continue driving through the park to a second parking/picnic area next to an old brick water treatment facility. Park here.

The Hike

Before starting on your walk, take a minute to read the display on the lawn of the water treatment plant, and look at the old photographs of its building and the turn-of-the-century era when Fort Collins used the facility to clean its water. The facility was closed in 1987 when the city outgrew the plant's capacity.

Then cross a gated bridge over the Poudre River, enjoying views of the steep, almost gothic canyon walls along this stretch of a "Wild and Scenic River." (For more about this designation, see the history section at the front of the book.) A visit in the autumn is a marvelous experience when the narrow leaf cottonwoods light up with gold. But anytime of year will provide its treasures: wild roses in the early summer, clematis and chokecherry blossoming in midsummer and vivid yellow rabbit brush in bloom in late summer and early fall. Walk along the road as it follows the river a short distance, watching carefully for a trail fork marked "Black Powder Trail" with a wooden sign directing you up a single-track trail into rocky terrain. The sign also mentions the Picnic Rock Burn of 2004 which left scars along sections of the trail you are about to explore.

I must quibble with the park folks' designation of the trail as "easy/moderate." The first section of trail in particular shimmies along crumbly cliff face and is not for the feint at heart, although it is still a well-constructed and manageable route. Quickly, however, the path winds its way up a cool ponderosa draw where you will see your first signs of the burn. One face of the trees' trunks are blackened where the fire sucked its way down the draw. However, the maturity of the ponderosas in this lush spot no doubt protected them well. Other trees, limber pines above, didn't fair so well, as you can see as you come up on the ridge and look down canyon.

From here, the trail rides the backbone of a high ridge up toward a pinnacle that is not technically the summit of the Poudre Canyon itself. As you walk, you'll see vast undulations of canyon wall before and beyond you in every direction. A truly unique hiking experience as most trails in the canyon stick to water draws and rarely climb the walls themselves. (**Mount McConnel** is another exception.) From the precipice point, a flattish rock outcropping, I had the feeling I could drop a lucky penny straight down into the river, there's that much of a projection above the river and highway below. A great spot to sit with a pair of binoculars and watch for bighorn sheep or raptors. From here, return the way you came.

When you get back down to the road, you may decide to explore the road further up along the river, scouting for quiet shady spots along the banks where pink rock reflects in still pools. By following this road and veering left over a bridge, you can make your way up to the Seaman Dam (owned by the City of Greeley). A steep climb up to an enforcement wall offers views of the reservoir nestled amongst the shaggy hills at 5,478 feet.

While the word is slowly but surely getting out about the new Gateway Mountain Park, amazingly, I found the area relatively serene on my visit. The picnic areas at the parking area provide lots of shade and several shelters are available for larger groups.

 Greyrock Summit Trail #946

▶ **4 miles one way** ▶ **Strenuous**

Maps: U.S.G.S. Poudre Park

Beginning Elevation: 5,558 feet

Ending Elevation: 7,613 feet

Access Road: Paved highway

Season: Year-round, depending on weather

Connector Trails: Greyrock Meadow Loop

Highlights: A northern Colorado hiking classic offering a little of everything—waterfalls, rock formations, a trip through multiple life zones. A very popular trail at all times of the year.

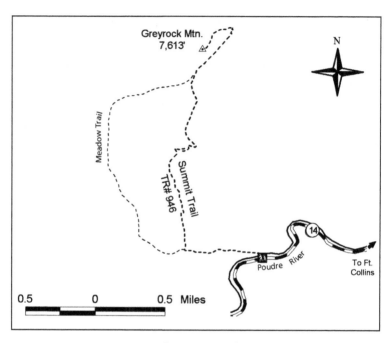

Greyrock Summit Trail #946

To Get There

From Ted's Place (junction of 287 and 14), take Highway 14 up the Poudre Canyon 8 miles to the Greyrock parking area. The turnoff is well posted. You've driven too far if you reach the town of Poudre Park. If the parking lot is full (and it could be at any time of year due to the popularity of this destination), several roadside spots are available on either side of the highway.

The Hike

After crossing the highway and the footbridge over the Cache la Poudre River, the trail leads up through a tunnel of chokecherry bushes and then on into ponderosas, junipers, and yuccas along a creek bed.

Greyrock Mountain

During winter months, the creek is often just a trickle, but it can rage in the spring runoff. At the 1-mile point, the trail forks right toward Greyrock Mountain and left on the **Greyrock Meadow Loop.** Toward the top of the gulch, past the tumbling waterfalls, red-barked ponderosa pines beckon with their scent. Some say the mature ponderosa pine exudes the smell of vanilla or butterscotch—you choose your flavor.

Toiling out of the gulch becomes a more strenuous task, but plentiful switchbacks make the going easier. On the side of the south-facing canyon wall, the terrain becomes noticeably more arid. Yuccas cling to the rocky mountainside, and massive boulders lean perilously out into the altitudes. But, wow, the views! I have classified this trail as strenuous due to the tricky stepping required up this stretch of trail over a crumbly foot path.

The giant Greyrock itself, invisible from the highway, makes its grand appearance as you reach the top of the gulch, its circus-tent shaped head soaring into the blue when you least expect it. In certain light, the rock looks mossy green rather than gray. At the top of the gorge, an open meadow with a log bench in the shade of the pines monopolizes the best view of the rock and is one of the most sought-after picnic spots in northern Colorado. It is also a trail connection with the Greyrock Meadow Loop trail. To reach the meadow and its panoramic views of the mountain is only a short 1-mile side trip.

To reach the rock's summit, prepare for a bit of rock climbing. The ascent is not for the faint-hearted, as it requires plenty of hand-over-foot action (but no special gear). From the trail connection, head east, following signs to the summit. The views as you climb are remarkable. You can see Lory State Park's red sandstone hogbacks holding back Horsetooth Reservoir, with Fort Collins beyond. Unfortunately, the skyline into the eastern plains, which once offered the nature lover the sensation of endlessness, is becoming increasingly smudged with the gloom of smog.

The last section of trail requires following cairns (rock piles) over the terrain dominated by stone to reach the summit. Nestled into the cap of rock is a Shangri-la, an oasis complete with a sampling of pine, aspen, and spruce trees and, farther along, Greyrock Lake, a pool of water reflecting the bizarre rock landscape around it. Please resist the temptation to impact this sensitive and unique spot further by camping here and especially by burning campfires. Fires blacken and deface the beautiful colors of the rocks—a form of graffiti.

Greyrock Meadow Loop

▶ 6.75-mile loop   ▶ Strenuous

Maps: U.S.G.S. Poudre Park

Beginning Elevation: 5,558 feet

Ending Elevation: 6,960 feet

Access Road: Paved highway

Season: Year-round, depending on weather

Connector Trails: Greyrock Summit Trail #946

Highlights: Alternate route to a famous rock mountain by way of a
    unique meadow. Unbeatable views.

To Get There

From Ted's Place (junction of 287 and 14), take Highway 14 up the
Poudre Canyon 8 miles to the Greyrock parking area. The turnoff is well
posted. If the parking lot is full (and it could be at any time of year due
to the popularity of this destination), several roadside spots are available
on either side of the highway. You've gone too far if you reach the town
of Poudre Park.

The Hike

This hike makes a good alternate route, a little longer and only
slightly less strenuous than **Greyrock Summit Trail #946,** to Greyrock
Mountain. Keep in mind, either route you choose, that no camping is
allowed within 0.25 mile of the trail or along the first 0.5 mile. Also,
please be sure to break down all fire rings, and practice the leave-no-

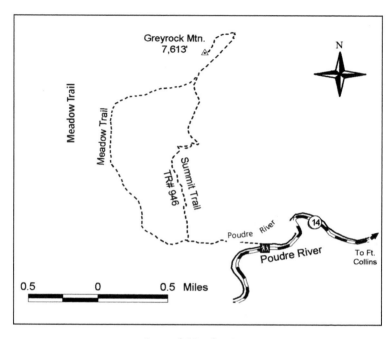

Greyrock Meadow Loop

trace camping style. The summit of Greyrock is beginning to show its popularity by the debris people leave behind.

From the parking area, cross the highway and then a footbridge over the Poudre River. The first mile of the trail weaves through a green, humid tunnel of chokecherry bushes that, in their spring bloom, look and smell something like a wild white lilac bush. A welcome greeting to the mountains.

At a trail fork at 1 mile, follow signs left to Greyrock Meadow (right heads up **Greyrock Summit Trail #946**). The chokecherry bushes dominate the trail until the draw begins to steepen. Here the path switchbacks up the canyon wall into the mountain mahogany brush. Much of the hike is through open brush hillsides with little shade. Carry plenty of water. For the climb to the shoulder of the ridge that will take

Greyrock Mountain above its meadow

you to the top, the trail ascends out of the creek drainage, making a giant
S-shaped switchback. You will have magnificent views of the Poudre
Canyon and its high country from an overlook. From another overlook
near the top of the draw are more views, this time into **Hewlett Gulch**
and the Red Feather area beyond. The trail cuts across the ridge for your
first views of Greyrock Mountain. Soon the trail descends into the large
grassy meadow just northwest of the peak.

Greyrock Meadow is a special spot, fringed with granite outcroppings
and wild iris. The Summit Trail is the direct route to the top, but the
Meadows Loop is what a friend of mine would call the "eye candy" route,
taking its time to go the extra mile for the best vistas. If you come in the
early hours of the morning or as the sun sets, you may spy deer grazing
on the lush meadow grasses. Views of Greyrock from the meadow are
some of the finest.

To continue the loop, follow the path around the periphery of the meadow and up to the foot of Greyrock where the trail intersects the Summit Trail. From here you can choose to climb the mountain (see **Greyrock Summit Trail #946**) or descend to your car via the Summit Trail, which returns by way of a drainage parallel to the one you hiked in on. The total distance of the loop is 6.75 miles.

Hewlett Gulch Trail #947

▶ **4.25 miles one way**   ▶ **Moderate**

Maps: U.S.G.S. Poudre Park

Beginning Elevation: 5,687 feet

Ending Elevation: 6,400 feet

Access Road: Paved highway

Season: Year-round, depending on weather

Connector Trails: Two different possible loops

Highlights: Remnants of old homesites and mine tailings at an easy distance up one of the grander gulches of Poudre Canyon.

To Get There

From Ted's Place (junction of 287 and 14), take Highway 14 up the Poudre Canyon 10 miles. At the sign for Hewlett Gulch, turn right onto a small road over a bridge. The road leads past homes to a large parking area with restrooms available.

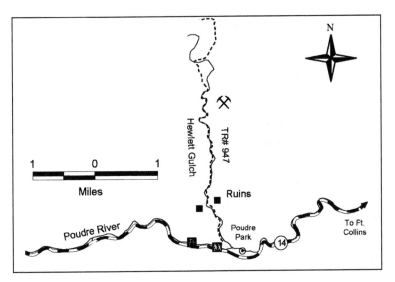

Hewlett Gulch Trail #947

The Hike

After walking across the bridge over the Poudre River, be sure to stay on the road past the homes on the right and the distance across private property (0.25 mile). Beware of the superfriendly dogs living at the home near the forest boundary. They're bound to decide to venture along with you. (What a life!)

The trail is very open and broad at its beginning, giving the trekker the opportunity to see the cliff-bedecked gulch from a distance. As you circumvent these canyon walls, keep your eyes to the skies for hawks and bighorn sheep that live in the highest rocks. At mile 1, watch for an old foundation and standing fireplace in the low-hung shade of a large cottonwood. The homesite can't be too ancient due to the use of cinder block and concrete, but it's a nice spot to sit and imagine life in the canyon country as a permanent resident. A second red rock foundation can be found right by the trail a little farther along. If you visit during the warmest summer months, expect to see some orange poppies in bloom, left over from someone's garden. The canyon is named after Horace Huleatt, who lived somewhere along it in the late 1870s (the spelling was later changed to Hewlett for unknown reasons). It was also part of the old Ute Trail and the site of a major archaeological find known as the Gordan Creek burial. Forest Service employees accidentally discovered the ceremonial grave of a Paleo-Indian woman dated 7700 B.C., one of the few Paleo-Indian sites found in the United States.

Many creek crossings are necessary on the Hewlett Gulch Trail, no easy task during the spring runoff. The trail soon ascends into the upper montane life zone, with ponderosas and a few Douglas firs replacing the rare juniper found at the beginning stretch of trail. Soon after, a wide-open meadow at the foot of a majestic rocky peak provides more opportunities for wildlife viewing. Look for old mine tailings, an unusual ochre color, spilling down the canyon wall at 2.75 miles. At a three-way trail fork immediately after the mine, I recommend staying right and then right again, sticking with the creek as it carves its way into the narrowing box canyon where you can get face-to-face with the geology of the gulch.

Hewlett Gulch is a favorite with mountain bikers, who have extended the trail farther than shown on most maps. Also, because of the good deer forage in the gulch, deer hunters, some on all-terrain vehicles (ATVs), are regular visitors here in the fall, so come prepared with an orange vest during that season. At 4.25 miles, after the first really strenuous climb of the walk, the trail summits on top of a great wavy plateau with 360-degree views. Be ready for the shock of hiking all this way, only to find many private homes built up here. Although I recommend returning the way you came (the trail becomes hard to keep track of beyond this point), the trail does make a long loop back to the trail fork previously mentioned.

Mount McConnel Trail #801

▶ **4 miles round trip** ▶ **Moderate**

Maps: U.S.G.S. Big Narrows

Beginning Elevation: 6,720 feet

Ending Elevation: 8,000 feet

Access Road: Paved highway

Connector Trails: Kreutzer Nature Trail

Season: Year-round, depending on weather

Highlights: Interpretive nature walk through mature ponderosa pine forest, Poudre Canyon vistas, and opportunities for wildlife viewing.

To Get There

From Ted's Place (junction of 287 and 14), take Highway 14 up the Poudre Canyon 22 miles to Mountain Park Campground. Cross the bridge over the Poudre River and follow signs to the trailhead by staying right and continuing to the back of the parking area where several information signs designate the trailhead. Park and walk beyond these signs.

The Hike

The hike begins by traversing the upper level of Mountain Park Campground, a sprawling, paved, and very popular destination for campers and picnickers alike. For those in search of an authentic wilderness experience, this sort of glamour can be a bit daunting. (Unfortunately, in the past few years, much of Poudre Canyon has seen

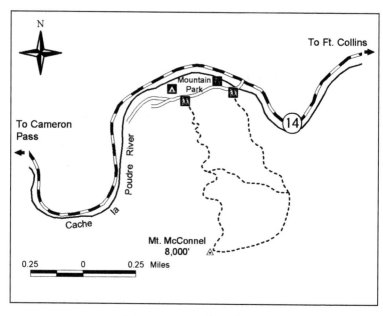

Mount McConnel Trail #801

its bends and twists paved over to make room for more visitors.) But don't turn back. Better sights await. Although Mount McConnel and its trail can be overrun with people on the weekends during peak tourist season, at midweek the Summit Trail holds promise of some solitude, even in August, and off-season is an even better time.

The 2-mile Kreutzer Trail, shorter but equally as strenuous as the Summit Trail, is an interpretive loop with posted plaques along the way that provide information about the ponderosa pine habitat. Each plaque is worth a stop. The Forest Service has done a fine job of including everything from local bird life to how talus slopes form. The trail is named after the first forest ranger of the Roosevelt Forest, a man who later became the supervisor in 1921. Because the trail covers land inside the Cache la Poudre Wilderness Area, no mountain bikes are allowed.

Along the Mount McConnel Trail

The trail ascends through ponderosa pine, juniper, and Douglas fir with bitterbrush and mountain mahogany forming the thick understory. It is 1 mile to the junction of the Kreutzer interpretive trail, but even if you intend to do only the shorter loop, it's worth continuing another 0.25 mile past the fork to a spectacular overlook of the river with a vertical rock formation close at hand. Although the Kreutzer Nature Walk provides excellent wildlife information, the Summit Trail has a monopoly on the best vistas.

Wild geranium is a lavender color at this lower level of the Poudre Canyon. (At higher elevations, such as among the aspen groves of **Roaring Creek,** the flower is usually white.) You will also notice spiky yucca plants growing along the trail to the summit of Mount McConnel. Perhaps the most majestic viewpoint along either trail comes at 1.5 miles. Spider-webbing side canyons lead the eye into the distance for a glimpse of the snowy Mummy Range. Watch and listen for hawks soaring below you.

At the top, the views are limited due to tree coverage. Trees appear to grow right out of the large rocks crusting the summit of this mountain. The descent, although steep and cumbersome in spots, is a rugged and beautifully authentic canyon country experience, enjoyable for the variety of boulders and grassy hillsides. As the trail approaches the thundering river, you pass through a lush, darker forest before emerging near the bridge at the head of the parking lot.

Young Gulch Trail #837

▶ **4.75 miles one way** ▶ **Easy**

Maps: U.S.G.S. Poudre Park

Beginning Elevation: 5,800 feet

Ending Elevation: 7,080 feet

Access Road: Paved highway, good gravel road last 500 yards

Season: Year-round, depending on weather

Connector Trails: None

Highlights: This hike, just 12 miles up the Poudre Canyon, offers a pleasant creek-side stroll with lots of small waterfalls, spectacular geology, and meadows tucked among the rolling hills.

To Get There

From Ted's Place (junction of 287 and 14), take Highway 14 up the Poudre Canyon 12 miles to the Ansel Watrous Campground, located soon after the Diamond Rock picnic area. You've gone too far if you make it to Mishawaka. There is no road sign, but a Roosevelt National Forest trailhead sign is visible from the highway. Drive about 500 feet up a dirt access road to the parking area.

The Hike

From the parking area, the views of Young Gulch and its towering reddish canyon walls are at their best. Young Creek is a small tributary of the Cache la Poudre River. This walk rarely strays from the side of the stream, so be prepared for many crossings. In the spring runoff when the snows have been good, footing can get tricky. The walk is charming and

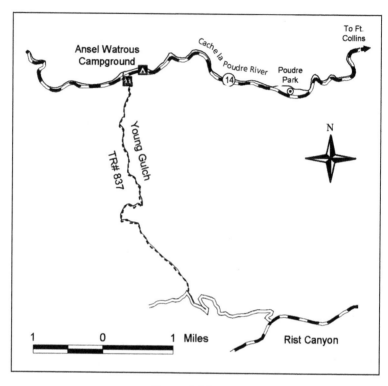

Young Gulch #837

cool in midsummer, especially along the first section that ambles along under large shady narrowleaf cottonwoods, ponderosas, and junipers and makes frequent encounters with the creek, which pools reflectively beneath the granite walls of the canyon.

Although many small side paths tempt the trekker into hiker-made campsites, no camping is allowed along the first 2 miles or within a 0.25-mile radius of the trail.

The trail is relatively flat most of its distance, and you climb only a bit more strenuously as it ascends into some fascinating geology. The creek tumbles over the rocks dramatically with several small waterfalls along the way. Although a springtime visit means more difficult stream crossings, it is an enchanting time of year when butterflies of every color flutter above the path as you pass. In the midsection of the trail, aspen stands and grassy meadows appear around each bend as the canyon widens. Ahead, the rock walls retreat, and the route leads into denser coniferous forest.

This trail has not been fully discovered by the mountain biking crowd, perhaps because of the number of creek crossings or the lack of exciting climbs and descents. However, mountain biking is allowed on the Young Gulch Trail.

The upper stretches of the trail break onto panoramic views of the shaggy higher-altitude mountains and surrounding area. Up here, the trail winds through large mullein and sunflower meadows, and the creek shrinks to little more than a meandering trickle.

The trail's terminus comes after you climb the first steep hill of the entire route, summiting a high spot on a rock outcropping overlooking a private cabin and someone's private property and a 4WD road off Rist Canyon Road below. (Some lucky person has a private backyard trailhead.) You would have to trespass on private property to access Young Gulch from the Rist Canyon end. Even from the top, the views of Young Gulch are limited due to heavy tree cover.

UPPER POUDRE CANYON

Some of the wildest stretches of the Cache la Poudre River can be found as it roars off the mountains of its origin. The landscape is dominated by Engelmann spruce, subalpine fir, and lodgepole pine forests that hide high mountain lakes and sprawling parks. Hiking destinations such as **Lulu City, Mirror Lake,** and Thunder Pass provide backdoor accesses into Rocky Mountain National Park (backcountry permits are required for overnight camping); other trails such as **Zimmerman Lake, Big South,** and **Trap Park** lie inside or on the outskirts of vast wildernesses. The area is managed by Roosevelt National Forest, which enforces a dog-leash law.

Historically, the area was dominated by the legendary presence of the Zimmerman family. John Zimmerman owned and operated the famous Keystone Hotel and resort in the late 1800s and homesteaded much of the high country along the Poudre Canyon's upper reaches. The Keystone Hotel, which was torn down to make way for the fish hatchery near Rustic, was a full-scale monument of its time, with a ballroom, billiard room, and grand piano. **Zimmerman Lake** was owned by the family until well into the 1900s and was a favorite family fishing spot. After their father's death in 1917, his daughters, Eda and Aggie, ran the hotel on their own. After Eda's death, Aggie (the namesake of **Lake Agnes**) lived for years in a cabin at Kinikinik in the winter and at another cabin on Chambers Lake in the summer.

The fact that Highway 14 over Cameron Pass wasn't paved into North Park until 1978 is evidence of how impenetrable and wild-spirited the high country is above Poudre Canyon.

Big South Trail #944: Lower

▶ **6.75 miles one way**   ▶ **Moderate**

Maps: U.S.G.S. Boston Peak, Chambers Lake

Beginning Elevation: 8,438 feet

Ending Elevation: 9,280 feet

Access Road: Paved highway

Season: Early summer to fall

Connector Trails: Flowers Trail #939

Highlights: This access to the Big South Trail provides an authentic canyon experience along the headwaters of the Poudre River.

To Get There

From Ted's Place (junction of 287 and 14), take Highway 14 up the Poudre Canyon 44 miles to the Big South trailhead and campground about 1 mile after Poudre Falls. If you reach the Aspen Glen Campground, you've gone too far. Parking is somewhat limited.

The Hike

This is one of two accesses to the Big South Trail; the upper stretch of trail is described as a separate hike in this book. The two sections of the trail were once connected by a footbridge over the Poudre River upstream. The bridge was washed out, and the Forest Service does not intend to rebuild it any time soon. The only way to cross the river is by wading or rock hopping when it is at its very lowest, and you shouldn't count on accessing the full length of the Big South Trail. This makes **Big South Upper** a bit more secluded. Opportunities for solitude are not as

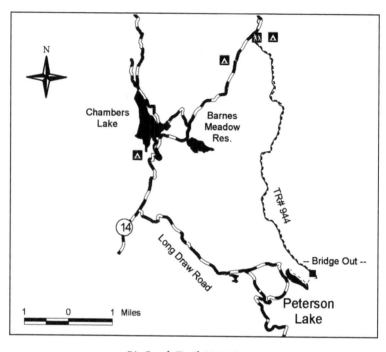

Big South Trail #944: Lower

good on the Highway 14 access, as it is a popular day-hiking and fishing destination.

The name Big South Fork is used to distinguish this part of the Poudre River from the South Fork, which drains out of Pingree Park, and from the North Fork, which pours off the Red Feather area to join the other two on the plains. The Big South Fork starts in Rocky Mountain National Park at Poudre Lake, carving its way down through the stone to form a dramatic canyon, a northern Colorado treasure that reminds us of what all of Poudre Canyon must have once been like before roads and development encroached.

The views of the Big South canyon are enticing from the parking area. Walk past the trailhead displays under the aspens. (This is a

Along Big South Trail #944: Lower

good hike for seeing the autumn colors at their best.) The trail enters the Comanche Peak Wilderness Area at 0.5 mile, and beyond here, no mechanized travel, including mountain bikes, is allowed. The trail tracks the broad river, providing fishing access among the willows and alders. Even at this altitude, the river is impressive in width and depth. By mile 2, the canyon walls have met the trail, and trekkers must cross a talus slope and climb a steep but short ridge for majestic views of the upper and lower reaches of Big South canyon.

From here the trail maintains its altitude above the confined space of the canyon below. The walk leads you through mixed forests of aspens, spruces, and firs to connect with the Flowers Trail where the washed-out bridge once led over the river to Peterson Lake.

Big South Trail #944: Upper

▶ 4.25 miles one way   ▶ Moderate

Maps: U.S.G.S. Chambers Lake

Beginning Elevation: 10,076 feet

Ending Elevation: 9,280 feet

Access Road: Good gravel road last 8.5 miles, all cars

Season: Midsummer to fall

Connector Trails: Mirror Lake Trail, Rocky Mountain National Park access, Peterson Lake Trail

Highlights: This stretch of the Big South offers solitude among expansive views with wild waterfalls and fishing opportunities.

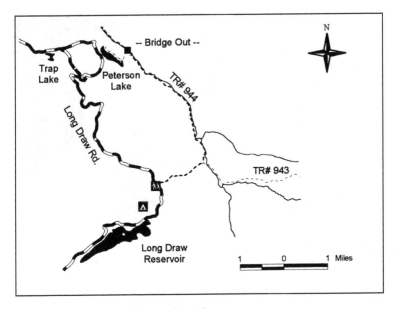

Big South Trail #944: Upper

To Get There

From Ted's Place (junction of 287 and 14), take Highway 14 up the Poudre Canyon 50.5 miles to the Long Draw Road turnoff (across the highway from the **Blue Lake** trailhead). Drive along the good gravel road, continuing past the Peterson Lake fork, 8.75 miles to the Corral Creek trailhead on the left, located just before the Long Draw Reservoir Campground. You'll find ample parking and a ranger station at the trailhead.

The Hike

This is one of two accesses to the Big South Trail; the second one is described as a separate hike (**Big South Trail #944: Lower**). The two sections of the trail were once connected by a footbridge over the Poudre River 4.25 miles downstream. The bridge was washed out, and the Forest

The author and her dog enjoy the mists of a large waterfall on the Big South Trail #944: Upper

Service does not intend to rebuild it any time soon. The only way to cross the river is by wading or rock hopping when it is at its very lowest, and you shouldn't count on accessing the full length of the Big South Trail. This means that the upper section is a bit more secluded than the section accessed by Highway 14.

From the parking area, walk past the trailhead display and along an old overgrown road as it descends through spruce and fir forest, with little Corral Creek burbling down a draw below. Continue on the Corral Creek Trail 1 mile to the junction with the Big South Trail where you head north (left), veering downstream along the Big South Fork of the Poudre River. The name Big South Fork distinguishes this section of the Poudre River from the South Fork, which drains out of Pingree Park, and from the North Fork, which drains out of the Red Feather area. The Big South

Fork starts in Rocky Mountain National Park as a small tricklet emptying from Poudre Lake. But by the time it leaves the national park, it is by no means small. Along this section of the trail, the river is much the same width as at the lower section but is more torrential, plunging over sheer drops in a spray of mist. However, the geology along this section is gentler, the gorge walls rolling along its length, black with conifers, with occasional glimpses of the high summits towering just beyond sight.

After the trail fork, follow rock cairns across riverside meadows abloom with wildflowers in midsummer. Along a stretch of the river beyond the 2-mile point, watch for (or better yet, listen for) two different waterfalls tumbling over the rocks a short distance from trailside. They are approximately 0.25 mile apart, each dramatic in its own way. The first competes with Poudre Falls off Highway 14 for sheer drop, whereas the second carves a fascinating channel through the granite to create a large, reflective green pool below.

Many spots along this upper stretch of the Big South are prized fishing holes, and most hikers I saw were carting a fishing pole to attempt to catch the endangered greenback cutthroat trout harbored in these waters. The greenback cutthroat is native to the eastern slope drainages, including the Poudre River (but, interestingly, not to the western slope drainages).

The waterfalls are a destination in themselves, but the trail continues on a ridge above the river through dense forest to intercept the Peterson Lake Trail at 4.75 miles. You could leave a second car here to make a two-car shuttle out of the trip.

Lulu City

▶ 2.5 miles one way   ▶ Moderate

Maps: U.S.G.S. Fall River Pass

Beginning Elevation: 10,175 feet

Ending Elevation: 9,360 feet

Access Road: Good gravel road last 10 miles

Season: Midsummer to fall

Connector Trails: Trail continues through to a second trailhead on Trail Ridge Road. Also accesses Thunder Pass, Big Dutch Creek, and Skeleton Gulch Trails.

Highlights: This backdoor access into Rocky Mountain National Park crosses the Colorado River at its headwaters before taking you to a historic ghost town.

To Get There

From Ted's Place (junction of 287 and 14), take Highway 14 up the Poudre Canyon 50.5 miles to the Long Draw Road turnoff, between Chambers Lake and Joe Wright Reservoir. Follow signs past the turnoff to Peterson Lake toward Long Draw Reservoir. There are many campsites along the way, and a campground is at the reservoir. Drive past the reservoir to the Never Summer trailhead. Long Draw Road dead-ends in the parking lot.

The Hike

The trail immediately meets up with a gravel road following the Grand Ditch drainage. Although the road itself isn't particularly

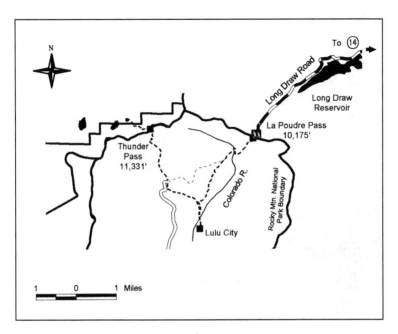

Lulu City

picturesque, the views from it are outstanding. You will encounter a chain strung across the road with a sign informing hikers that dogs and motorized vehicles are not allowed in the park. Take my advice and leave the pooch at home when hiking into Rocky Mountain National Park. Fines are steep, and there is a ranger station located at the bridge across the drainage ditch.

Rounding the ridge, you'll break out onto a beautiful view of Thunder Pass and Mount Richthofen (elevation 12,940 feet). Tepee Mountain, Lead Mountain, and Cirrus Mountain loom more distantly. A small dam leads off the Grand drainage and forks down the hillside into the canyon you'll soon be hiking. This dam marks the Continental Divide, and the waters here will eventually flow into the North Fork of the Colorado River.

View of the valley where Lulu City once prospered

At 1 mile, you will notice two wooden trail signs, one directing you up the road toward Thunder Pass and the other designating the route into the trees to Lulu City. (A second sign is posted for Thunder Pass at the 2.5-mile point, just beyond some maintenance buildings.) Take the trail down into the spruce and fir forest, following signs to Lulu City whenever necessary.

The trail wanders pleasantly through the forest before breaking out onto a steep cliff overlooking the North Fork of the Colorado River and some astonishing rock formations and spires. The trail continues descending (but on the return trip you'll be surprised to find it isn't uncomfortably steep) with sweeping views before you. The trail is maintained extremely well, with every stream crossed by a walking bridge or leveled log. One of these small streams is the Colorado River at its headwaters, a river that provides water to a number of U.S. states and Mexico.

As you continue hiking, keep your eyes on the valley below. At one point, a perfect view opens out onto the valley where Lulu City once reigned. As you emerge from the forest into this valley, you'll find yourself in a parklike area, the river nearby. Begin looking for remnants of old Lulu City here. There's not much left but rotted foundations of old log buildings, but the sleuthing is fun. Lulu City was founded in 1879 by either Benjamin Franklin Burnett or Captain Yankee (no one is sure), but the town was named after Burnett's daughter. The town was planned to last longer than its three or four years, but by 1883 only the diehards were left. Built on a grid with 19 streets and 100 blocks and boasting four lumber mills, a luxury hotel, a post office, and a justice of the peace, the town might have survived had it not been for the high price of hauling and digging for the low-grade gold, silver, and lead mined in the area. The Old Flowers Road, now a long-distance hiking trail, was built to connect Lulu City to Fort Collins, but to no avail. At its height, Lulu City boasted a population of 500 citizens.

 Mirror Lake

▸ **6 miles one way**   ▸ **Moderate**

Maps: U.S.G.S. Chambers Lake, Comanche Peak
Beginning Elevation: 10,076 feet
Ending Elevation: 10,960 feet
Access Road: Good gravel road last 8.5 miles

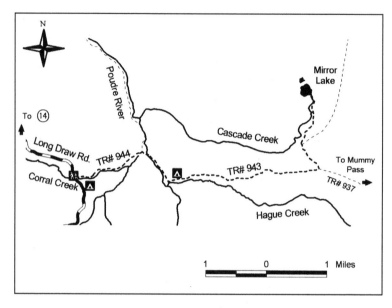

Mirror Lake

Season: Midsummer to fall

Connector Trails: Cache la Poudre River Trail, **Big South Trail,**
Mummy Pass Trail

Highlights: Rocky Mountain National Park access into a unique
cirque lake in an alpine basin with several waterfalls.

To Get There

From Ted's Place (junction of 287 and 14), take Highway 14 up the
Poudre Canyon 50.5 miles to Long Draw Road, a turnoff just across the
pavement from the **Blue Lake** trailhead. Continue on Long Draw Road
8.5 miles past the Peterson Road turnoff. The Corral Creek trailhead is
just before the Long Draw Campground. An information station is available across the road from the trailhead with trail maps of connecting
trails in the area.

Stormy weather descends on Mirror Lake

The Hike

Walk across the footbridge at the trailhead and proceed 1 mile to the junction with the **Big South Trail,** where you want to stay right following signs to Mirror Lake. The trail is wide and well groomed, with a footbridge over each stream crossing and signs at all trail connections. This first section of the walk is easy, rambling alongside Corral Creek, which drains into the Cache la Poudre River, before veering east. At 1.75 miles, the trail crosses Hague Creek and comes to the Hague campsite where a privy is provided. Cross the footbridge here and stay straight. (Turning right takes you to the campsite.) From the Hague Creek crossing, the trail begins to climb at a moderately strenuous incline through fine Engelmann spruce and subalpine fir forest. You will have occasional glimpses of the wide stream meadows below and, later, the Mummy Range, which will seem almost within your reach. At 4 miles, you reach the Mummy Pass Trail junction. Head north (left) into the basin where Mirror Lake lies. The Koenig campsite, a spacious spot with a hitching post for horses, is at the 5-mile point. Several campsites are also available just south of the lake and offer picturesque views of the waterfalls tumbling out of the cirque lake.

Mirror Lake is small and lives up to its name as long as the sun is shining. But count on afternoon rain showers every day in the summer months. The scree slopes surrounding the lake likely will be decked with snow year-round. Because Rocky Mountain National Park is so popular, you will have little opportunity for solitude on this hike.

Montgomery Pass Trail #977

▶ **1.5 miles one way**   ▶ **Strenuous**

Maps: U.S.G.S. Clark Peak

Beginning Elevation: 9,060 feet

Ending Elevation: 11,000 feet

Access Road: Paved highway

Season: Midsummer to fall

Connector Trails: Trail #977 continues north to connect with the Sawmill Creek Trail. Trail #981 (going south) accesses Diamond Peaks and Cameron Pass. A third option is to continue down a 4WD road into the State Forest.

Highlights: An old cabin site hidden among old-growth forest and views from an alpine pass looking down into Poudre Canyon and North Park.

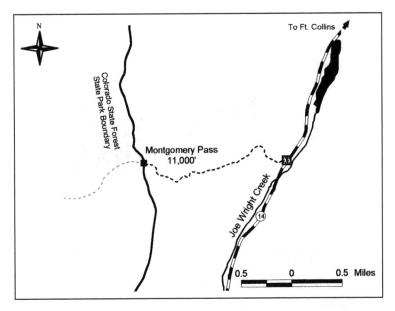

N

To Ft. Collins

Colorado State Forest
State Park Boundary

Montgomery Pass
11,000'

Joe Wright Creek

14

0.5   0   0.5 Miles

Montgomery Pass Trail #977

To Get There

From Ted's Place (junction of 287 and 14), take Highway 14 up the Poudre Canyon 53.5 miles to the **Zimmerman Lake** trailhead, where you'll find a large parking lot and restrooms. Park in the lot and walk across the highway to the trailhead, which is identified by a large wooden informational display.

The Hike

Get an early start for this destination. The hike will take you into the tundra, well above timberline where summer lightning storms can strike suddenly.

From the trailhead, the path wanders alongside Montgomery Creek a short distance before skirting uphill at a steady climb. The trail is wide and clearly defined due to its year-round popularity. The forest is old-

Montgomery Pass

growth Engelmann spruce and subalpine fir, some so large you couldn't get your arms around them. Just before the trail reaches timberline, you'll find the site of a run-down cabin, possibly an old line cabin that cowboys used while watching over their cattle when they moved them to the high country in the summer. The cabin overlooks breathtaking views of Poudre Canyon. Wander around a bit here, noticing the hole in the ground where a root cellar might have once been. It must have been an extraordinary experience to live in such a place all summer.

Beyond the cabin, alpine meadows open out to more views. The trail disappears for a few hundred yards, overgrown with flowers, but if you look up at the saddle, you can see the wooden sign and hike toward it. It gets cold and windy at the pass, but as you climb over the crest, your efforts are rewarded with views into North Park and the Never Summer Range. From Montgomery Pass, you can see the Diamond Peaks to your south; the body of water visible below is North Michigan Reservoir.

Hikes Around Fort Collins

If you are backpacking through this area, please remember that alpine meadows are their own delicately balanced ecosystem. Try to stay on the trail as much as possible, and tear down all fire rings or use one left by a previous visitor. Because this hike is accessible from the highway, opportunities for solitude are low.

Roaring Creek Trail #952

▶ 4.5 miles one way   ▶ Moderate

Maps: U.S.G.S. Kinikinik, Boston Peak

Beginning Elevation: 7,740 feet

Ending Elevation: 9,880 feet

Access Road: Paved highway

Season: Early summer to fall

Connector Trails: 4WD Forest Road #517

Highlights: Views of Poudre Canyon with waterfalls and wildflowers in abundance.

To Get There

From Ted's Place (junction of 287 and 14), take Highway 14 up the Poudre Canyon 38 miles to the Roaring Creek trailhead, which is diagonal from the old Kinikinik Trading Post. The trail begins at the back of the parking area.

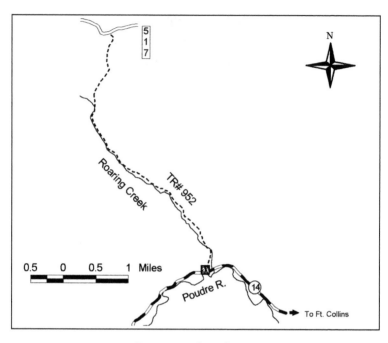

Roaring Creek Trail #952

The Hike

This hike provides one of the most superb examples of northern Colorado's natural diversity, the perfect place to bring a visitor who has had no experience of our wild places. From the parking lot, it looks as if the hike will be a walk through rock and juniper, even some yucca, a desertlike landscape. Indeed, this is the setting during the moderately strenuous ascent along Roaring Creek until you reach the footbridge at 0.25 mile. After you cross the thundering creek (Roaring Creek is a well-deserved name for all the waterfalls), the trail switchbacks upward into aspen and sagebrush with some fine views of Poudre Canyon. The many colorful wildflowers here are a midsummer surprise. Harebell, wild rose, purple alpine asters, pussytoes, yarrow, Indian paintbrush, even the exotic sego lily (the Utah State flower), are among the canyon

BONNIE BUTLER

The trail through the aspens along Roaring Creek

wildflowers growing along Roaring Creek. The trail begins to level out, leaving switchbacks behind and entering a mature ponderosa pine forest where the big red jigsaw-barked trees grow widely spaced and broadly branched. Sniff the ponderosa pine's bark. The reddish bark of the mature ponderosa pine has a distinctive caramel or butterscotch scent. It is interesting to note the differences between this swath of ponderosa forest in comparison with the forest you enter soon after. Here the lodgepole pines grow uniformly tall and skinny and tightly spaced. A campsite is available along the side of the nearby creek.

The trail continues out to reveal panoramic views of the mountain walls surrounding a wide, willowy park encircled by aspens. Here Roaring Creek is not roaring at all but is shallow and quiet, and the path becomes swampy. To deter erosion, log footbridges have been provided. The trail continues 4.5 miles to intersect the Bald Mountain 4WD Road #517 in the Red Feather Lakes area; this route can provide opportunities for long backpacking trips, connecting **Killpecker Creek** or **North Lone Pine** Trails. For a moderately difficult day hike into a secluded mountain valley, I found it comfortable to turn back at 2.25 miles.

Trap Park Trail #866

▶ 2.25 miles one way   ▶ Moderate

Maps: U.S.G.S. Chambers Lake

Beginning Elevation: 9,975 feet

Ending Elevation: 10,600 feet

Access Road: Good gravel road last 3 miles

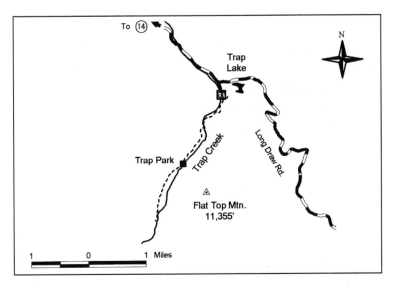

Trap Park Trail #866

Season: Midsummer to fall

Connector Trails: None

Highlights: Creek-side hike to high meadow park with expansive
views of the Neota Wilderness.

To Get There

From Ted's Place (junction of 287 and 14), take Highway 14 up the
Poudre Canyon 50.5 miles to Long Draw Road, between Chambers Lake
and Joe Wright Reservoir, across the road from the Blue Lake trailhead,
and continue 3 miles to the turnoff on the right to the Trap Park trailhead. Drive 0.25 mile into the parking area. No restrooms are available
at the trailhead.

The Hike

This destination, as well as its creek and lake, derives its name from the superb trapping once available here. During the early frontier days, the wide-open park at the foot of the Neota Wilderness was well known for its wildlife ripe for the pickings of such famous trappers as Robert Chambers (for whom Chambers Lake was named) and the French-Canadian Jacques Laramie in the employ of the Northwestern Fur Company (for whom the Laramie River and Fort Laramie were named). It's hard to imagine now the experience of seeing such an abundance of elk, beaver, bear, wolverine, and ptarmigan in this beautiful setting. Perhaps one day such a sight will exist again for our grandchildren to see.

The trail follows an old logging road, blocked off at the parking area. Walk beyond the roadblock and continue straight ahead. At a fork near the beginning of the trail, stay right. (The left-hand track winds into Trap Lake.) The climb is moderately strenuous, crossing wide swaths of talus slopes that make the trail rough walking. From here, the trail offers an excellent view of the lake and the surrounding high country. The creek can be heard roaring as it makes its way down the steep gorge below the trail, barely visible except for the glimpses of white water through the thick spruce forest.

The trail continues climbing steadily before encountering the Trap Creek crossing. Here the views open out onto panoramic vistas of Iron Mountain, and Trap Park lives up to its name, as spacious and grassy as any city park. There is no footbridge across the creek, which can be quite deep, deeper than it appears. The excellent views from beside the creek make this a nice picnic spot and turning-back point. However, if you choose to wade through, the trail continues another 1.75 miles to the foot of Iron Mountain.

The opportunity for wildlife viewing is excellent due to the proximity of high mountain country, stream, and forest. You have a good chance to observe a herd of elk or a moose grazing, but keep in mind that these animals of prey regard the human face as the face of a predator. Observe from a passive distance, allowing them to graze peacefully. This ensures that the herd will return year after year, proof that humanity can indeed share the wilderness with its permanent, wilder inhabitants. Trap Park makes a good launching-off point for further self-guided explorations into the Neota Wilderness.

48 Zimmerman Lake

▶ **1.5 miles one way** ▶ **Moderate**

Maps: U.S.G.S. Chambers Lake, Clark Peak

Beginning Elevation: 10,019 feet

Ending Elevation: 10,495 feet

Access Road: Paved highway

Season: Midsummer to fall

Connector Trails: None

Highlights: This ever-popular mountain lake destination offers views of the Neota Wilderness within easy access off Highway 14 near Cameron Pass.

To Get There

From Ted's Place (junction of 287 and 14), take Highway 14 up the Poudre Canyon 53.5 miles to the Zimmerman Lake parking area just below Cameron Pass at the far south end of Joe Wright Reservoir. Restrooms are available at the parking area. Park here and look for the trailhead information sign near the line of trees behind the restrooms.

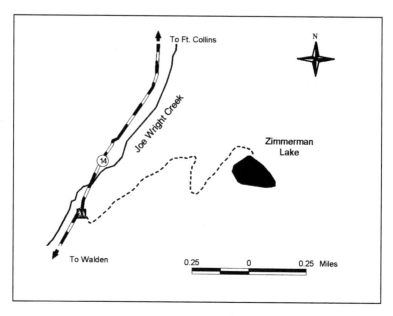

Zimmerman Lake

The Hike

The trail is a closed logging road that embarks from the south end of the parking area. If you're planning to fish, stop and read the fishing guidelines near the beginning of the trail concerning the reintroduction into Zimmerman Lake of greenback cutthroat trout and the egg-sampling project. The road heads uphill to the lake through subalpine firs. At a wide curve in the road, views open up behind you of the Cameron Pass area, with Cameron Peak visible to the northwest.

At the lake (a natural lake, although it has been reinforced to increase capacity), a sign informs anglers that only flies and lures can be used for fishing and all fish must be released. You can extend the walk by looping around the lake for closer views of the deep red volcanic ridge that looms above Zimmerman Lake's east shore. Even in the summertime,

Zimmerman Lake can get chilly winds, and it's best to take an extra jacket. The ridge lies within the Neota Wilderness, but the lake does not.

Zimmerman Lake was named after John Zimmerman, a homesteader who built and operated the famous Keystone Hotel a short way down the Poudre Canyon from 1893 until his death December 13, 1919, eleven days short of his eightieth birthday. The area Zimmerman Lake occupies was part of the family's first homestead and one of their favorite fishing holes. After their father's death, Agnes and Eda Zimmerman, his daughters, ran the hotel and retained the Zimmerman Lake property. **Lake Agnes,** on the other side of Cameron Pass at the foot of the Nokhu Crags, was named after Aggie Zimmerman by her father. The old Keystone Hotel was bought and torn down by the state in 1945 and a fish hatchery built in its place. Zimmerman Lake was passed down through the family until a land-trade agreement brought it into public hands in the late 1950s. Since then, it has become a popular recreational destination, summer and winter.

RAWAH WILDERNESS

"Rawah" is the name given to the area by the Native Americans (probably Arapaho) who roamed the region and means "wilderness," a slip of redundancy when the two words are strung together but expressive enough. The Rawah Wilderness is big country with multitudes of side trips and lakes and peaks to be discovered. The area is the headwaters of the Laramie River, which was named after Jacques Laramie, a trapper in the employ of the Northwest Fur Company who first hunted beaver here as early as 1820. As is true for many of the early trappers, the story of his death is the most fascinating part of his life. Ignoring the advice of his peers, Jacques returned to his cabin along the Laramie River even though he knew it was at the center of an Indian battleground. He was soon afterward found killed by Indians.

If you're interested in making a longer loop, I recommend doing a two-car shuttle, leaving a second vehicle at the Rawah trailhead and hiking in by way of the **West Branch Trail**, saving the more strenuous descent for the **Rawah Trail**. The Rawah Wilderness is a popular destination, and it's beginning to show some overuse. Try to practice low-impact camping, and consider choosing a campsite farther from the water's edge, where you may enjoy greater solitude as well. As is the case for most places in the Roosevelt National Forest, dogs must be kept on leashes in the Rawah Wilderness.

Blue Lake Trail #959

▶ **5.5 miles one way**   ▶ **Moderate**

Maps: U.S.G.S. Chambers Lake, Clark Peak

Beginning Elevation: 9,320 feet

Ending Elevation: 10,720 feet

Access Road: Paved highway

Season: Midsummer to fall

Connector Trails: West Branch Trail #960

Highlights: This popular four-seasons trail follows the Fall Creek
drainage around the backside of Cameron Peak to a cirque lake
located at the edge of timberline.

To Get There

From Ted's Place (junction of 287 and 14), take Highway 14 up the
Poudre Canyon 50.5 miles to the Blue Lake parking area directly across
the highway from the Long Draw Road turnoff and located between the
Chambers Lake turnoff and Joe Wright Reservoir.

The Hike

From the trailhead, walk past the informational display as the trail
winds down to cross Sawmill Creek over a large footbridge and up the
other side to follow a long ridge around into a second drainage (Fall
Creek). In mile 2, an overlook provides glimpsing views through the trees
of Chambers Lake, a large reservoir fed by Fall Creek. The trail winds
through lodgepole pines but is often shaded by deciduous alders as it
follows an old logging road.

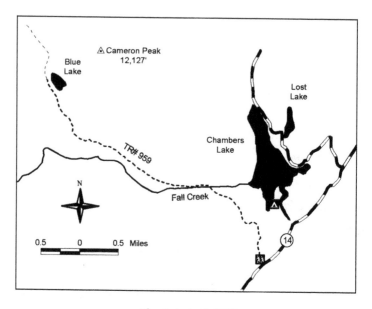

Blue Lake trail #959

Finally, the path crosses a second footbridge over Fall Creek and soon after meets the Rawah Wilderness boundary. From here, your climb is more strenuous, as the trail rambles through old-growth spruce and fir forest cluttered with underbrush and fallen timber. After climbing and descending through wild ravine country for several miles, you encounter some small meadows with views of Cameron Peak to the east, a large sprawling mountain with a steep red raw-looking summit. Cross a small footbridge and continue climbing on the last leg up to Blue Lake. A sign just before the lake reminds visitors that no camping or fires are allowed at Blue Lake, which lies at the edge of timberline. The lake is surrounded by steep slopes of brilliant wildflowers. To reach the lake's shore, watch for a side trail dropping down into the hollow where soaring walls of rock encircle the lake's west side. The main trail continues past the lake to a saddle at its north end, accessing the **West Branch Trail.** (The descent

Blue Lake

to the lake at its north end is difficult.) This saddle above the lake is a great launching-off spot for a climb up Cameron Peak (12,127 feet).

Views down into the crystal-clear water penetrate a vibrant green/blue lake worthy of its name. The lake provides good fishing with trout seeming to jump everywhere you look. Blue Lake is possibly the most popular Cameron Pass destination, with the exception of **Lake Agnes** or the **Big South Trail,** and thus you'll have few opportunities for solitude. In the summer season, even midweek, expect to share this beautiful place with day hikers, backpackers, and anglers alike.

Rawah Trail #961

▶ **8 miles one way**   ▶ **Strenuous**

Maps: U.S.G.S. Rawah Lakes

Beginning Elevation: 8,360 feet

Ending Elevation: 10,678 feet

Access Road: Good gravel road last 11 miles

Season: Midsummer to fall

Connector Trails: Camp Lakes Trail, Lost Lake Trail, Link Trail, McIntyre Trail, **West Branch Trail**

Highlights: Challenging trail into an area of multiple scenic lakes tucked under the watchful eyes of imposing mountain peaks.

To Get There

From Ted's Place (junction of 287 and 14), take Highway 14 up the Poudre Canyon 48.5 miles to the Laramie River Road turnoff to Glendevey. The turnoff is past the Aspen Glen Campground but before the Chambers Lake Road. Follow the maintained gravel road 11 miles around the north end of Chambers Lake, past the West Branch trailhead to the Rawah Trail parking area. Restrooms are available at the trailhead.

The Hike

From the parking area, cross the gravel road and follow a buck-and-rail fence past the dude ranch, proceeding through a fenced corridor beyond the private-property boundaries. A wide footbridge leads over the Laramie River. The trail meanders through lodgepole pine forest

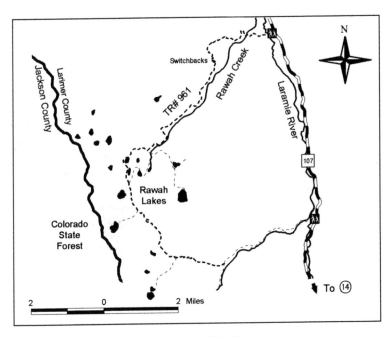

Rawah Trail #961

mixed with sunny stands of aspen, crossing Rawah Creek several times by way of footbridges. The third such bridge crosses just below a roaring waterfall about 2 miles into the hike. Beyond this point, the trail begins climbing in earnest through spacious coniferous forest. As you follow the trail along the course of Rawah Creek, you can hear but usually not see the water. You will switchback frequently to gain altitude above the gorge below. Once on top, the trail scurries along a ridgeline above the gorge. I characterize the trail as strenuous because of the rocky and difficult footing, reminiscent of finding your way along a dry riverbed.

You'll know you have completed about half the distance when you reach Half-Way Creek after climbing another series of switchbacks and crossing a medium-sized creek over a hand-hewn log bridge. Firs and spruces make this section of the trail a shady, streamside ramble,

View from the largest of the Rawah Lakes

and huckleberries carpet the forest floor in a soft green. A fork at 5.5 miles indicates the Lost Lake Trail, a side trail leading 1 mile to a small isolated lake and its subponds. After circling a large meadow identified as the Rawah Bog on many topographical maps, the trail begins its most difficult climb into the higher basins where the Rawah Lakes are nestled. This stretch is very rocky for a mile or so and takes the direct route to the top. You'll know you're past the worst when you encounter another meadow. Just beyond a footbridge onto the meadow, a side trail provides a nice place to take a breather and enjoy a small waterfall.

In approximately 0.75 mile from the Rawah Lakes, you'll observe signs to Camp Lakes, a 4.5-mile cutoff trail that connects to the **West Branch Trail** by way of two lakes on the east side of Sheep Mountain. (The last 1.5-mile descent off this connector trail is a real knee-buckler.)

The first of the Rawah Lakes is at the 8-mile point. Many backpackers make it this far and, exhausted from the climb in, search immediately for a campsite. But there are eight lakes in close proximity, most of them hidden among the evergreens and providing shelter and sensational views. Explore a bit farther from water's edge and you'll find the perfect spot. The Rawah Lakes are a popular backpacking and horsepacking destination, and many campsites have severe resource damage. Please abide by the signs and give these places time to regenerate. Little Rainbow Lake, at 10,838 feet, is above timberline and has very little by way of camping spots. Rawah Lakes #3 and #4 are each a mile farther south and just at or above timberline.

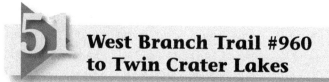

West Branch Trail #960 to Twin Crater Lakes

▶ 6.5 miles one way   ▶ Moderate

Maps: U.S.G.S. Boston Peak, Rawah Lakes

Beginning Elevation: 8,560 feet

Ending Elevation: 11,047 feet

Access Road: Good gravel road last 5.5 miles

Season: Midsummer to fall

Connector Trails: The **Rawah Trail** continues over Grassy Pass to Rawah Lakes, and the **West Branch Trail** continues to Island Lake. The Camp Lakes Trail makes a good connection route between the two.

Highlights: A hidden basin and its two lakes lie encircled by high mountain peaks and offer further opportunities for exploration.

To Get There

From Ted's Place (junction of 287 and 14), take Highway 14 up the Poudre Canyon 48.5 miles to the Laramie River Road turnoff to Glendevey. The turnoff is past the Aspen Glen Campground but before the Chambers Lake Road. Follow the maintained gravel road 5.5 miles around the north end of Chambers Lake to the West Branch trailhead parking lot. Restrooms are available at the trailhead.

The Hike

From the parking area, walk past the trailhead display sign and follow the trail as it leads back onto the road and over a bridge spanning

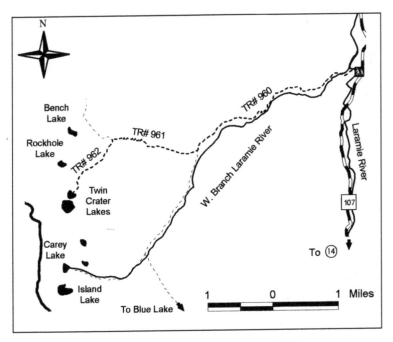

West Branch Trail #960 to Twin Crater Lakes

the Laramie River. After the bridge, watch for the path as it plunges into the willows and soon begins winding up through the aspens that flourish along the north wall above the gorge of the West Branch Fork of the Laramie River. For several miles, a soothing stroll leads through aspen country, and the going is moderately easy until after the Camp Lakes fork. (The Camp Lakes Trail is a strenuous climb for 1.5 miles before leveling off, accessing the Camp Lakes and serving as the **Rawah Trail** cutoff with some nice views of the Rawah Peaks. Total distance of the Camp Lakes Trail is about 4.5 miles, not counting the side trip to Upper Camp Lake.)

At 4.25 miles, the West Branch Trail veers off to the left, headed 2.5 miles farther in to access a side trail bound southward to **Blue Lake.** The West Branch Trail also ascends to Island, Carey, and Timber Lakes and

Rockhole Lake (in the foreground) with Twin Crater Lakes and Clark Peak visible beyond

their broad basin at the foot of Clark Peak where the fishing can be quite good. To continue on to Twin Crater Lakes, go right, following a sign along the Rawah Trail.

Beyond the trail fork, the route begins a series of switchbacks up through the darkening spruce and fir forest. Good log footbridges exist at all creek crossings over the North Fork of the Laramie River. Watch for a lovely multiple-tiered waterfall visible from trailside. You will meet the turnoff up to Twin Crater Lakes at 5.25 miles. The trail stair steps, climbing, plateauing, and climbing again to reach the Twin Crater basin. A long silver thread of a waterfall empties from these lakes, a welcome sight. Campsites are available on the bench near the lakes, but keep in mind the required setback from water's edge (100 feet, or 40 adult paces). The two lakes are separated only by a narrow land bridge. An unnamed hump shadows the basin to the south, while the craggy Snowbank Peak (12,322 feet) lords over the valley, decked in a permanent ice field. South Rawah Peak can be seen to the north with Rockhole and Bench Lakes capturing drainages on ledges to the north. (These lakes are not accessible by trail.) The Twin Crater Lakes basin makes the best jumping-off point for a strenuous ascent of South Rawah Peak, the highest of the two Rawahs at 12,644 feet. Look for a steep ridge above Rockhole Lake that leads to a false peak where you can undertake the final ascent to the north.

NORTH PARK AREA TRAILS

COLORADO STATE FOREST
STATE PARK

The largest of Colorado's state parks, this 71,000-acre tract within the Colorado State Forest stretches along the western slope of the Medicine Bow Range and offers some of northern Colorado's most famous hiking, including destinations such as **Lake Agnes** at the foot of the Nokhu Crags and **Ruby Jewel Lake** tucked under the arm of Clark Peak, the highest summit in North Park at 12,951 feet. The State Forest boasts miles of trail that lead through a diversity of ecosystems and offer plenty of opportunities for wildlife viewing. The State Forest provides a home for the highest density of moose in the region (indeed, Walden prides itself on being the moose-viewing capital of Colorado). Never Summer Nordic Yurts is a company that rents circular yurts, a kind of Mongolian canvas shelter, at several conveniently located spots throughout the State Forest; yurts can be used for winter or summer excursions. The company has a cabin with phenomenal views of the Nokhu Crags from the front door.

Mountain biking is allowed on most trails (except Lake Agnes) below timberline. No camping is allowed in the Lake Agnes basin, and the State Forest enforces a dog-leash law. Keep in mind that the Colorado State Forest State Park is a multimanaged area, meaning it is a school trust property administered by the State Land Board and is not strictly speaking public land. Be aware that logging and grazing occur throughout the park. The history of the State Forest is steeped in the lumber industry, and it's not unusual to come across old sawmill sites when hiking or skiing in the park. Watch for logging trucks on blind curves when driving the State Forest roads. The entrance fee into the State Forest State Park is $5 a day, but $55 annual passes can be purchased at the Moose Visitor Center and can be used to gain entrance into any of the forty-four state parks, including Lory State Park near Fort Collins.

To experience the State Forest fully requires a stop at the Moose Visitor Center, a favorite with kids. The interpretive displays at this visitor center are one of a kind, a treat for the old and young alike. (The visitor center is fully handicapped-accessible.) For more information about the park, contact the Colorado State Forest State Park at (970) 723-8366.

52 American Lakes

▶ **4 miles one way**   ▶ **Moderate**

Maps: U.S.G.S. Fall River Pass, Mount Richthofen

Beginning Elevation: 10,400 feet

Ending Elevation: 11,430 feet

Access Road: Good gravel road last 1.25 miles

Season: Midsummer to fall

Connector Trails: Thunder Pass Trail into Rocky Mountain National Park

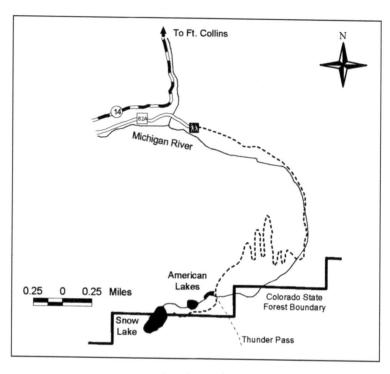

American Lakes

Highlights: Wildflower alpine meadows and three lakes at the foot of Nokhu Crags with the option to climb a high mountain pass for unsurpassed views.

To Get There

Take Highway 14 up the Poudre Canyon to the **Lake Agnes** turnoff about 2.25 miles west of Cameron Pass. At the entrance station at the bottom of the hill, stop and pay your $5 entry fee to the Colorado State Forest State Park, then drive 1.25 miles to the American Lakes trailhead. A designated campground (with a fee) is available on the road up to the Lake Agnes trailhead. No camping is allowed at the trailhead.

View of American Lakes from Snow Lake

The Hike

The trail begins by following an old logging road, and your walk is easy as the trail tracks the Middle Fork of the Michigan River that flows out of American Lakes to its source. This hike provides some of the finest opportunities I know of for wildflower identification as it climbs through life zones and finally above timberline into alpine tundra. At 1.5 miles, the trail meets the Michigan Ditch. (The road along the drainage is an excellent mountain biking road in the summer.) Cross the road and continue into the trees in the direction indicated by the sign.

At 2.5 miles, you will cross a footbridge over the creek, and the trail begins to climb steeply, hitting timberline soon after. In July and August, the wildflowers on these alpine slopes are dazzling. The Indian paintbrush blooms in every shade of red, pink, and deep magenta; it's small wonder that many Native American tribes living in the vicinity used it as a dye for fabrics. The bistort, arnica, elephant's head, and osha are also in ample supply. During the summer of 2001, the upper stretch of the trail was rerouted to include more switchbacks, a modification that makes the ascent less strenuous and less prone to erosion.

From the meadows, the trail continues to scale the hillside toward the basin where the lakes are tucked into the east side of the Nokhu Crags. The name "Nokhu" (pronounced NO-koo) is an Arapaho word meaning "eagle's nest." As I was looking up toward the jagged rock face, I noticed a lone rock perched in a niche that, silhouetted, struck me as exactly the shape of an eagle.

To reach the lakes, watch for an overgrown side trail leading down to their shores. The two American Lakes flow into one another with a narrow stretch to designate where one ends and the other begins. Sandbars in both lakes give them a gold ring around their perimeters. The main stem of the trail continues on to Thunder Pass for stirring views of Rocky Mountain National Park to the south and the Neota Wilderness to the east. Heed the name of this pass, and resist the urge to ascend if the weather becomes inclement. A trail continues over the pass to access the Grand Ditch Trail and **Lulu City**. Two camp sites are available among old-growth forest about 1 mile from the pass.

To reach Snow Lake at 11,430 feet, head for the cascade of water flowing off the rocky wall above American Lakes. This waterfall tumbles out of Snow Lake to feed the lower lakes. There is a rough hiker-made trail scaling the wall to the left side of the waterfall. Columbines, Colorado's lavender and white state flower, love the terracing created by all the rock. The climb to Snow Lake is less than 0.5 mile but is very strenuous. Because Snow Lake is completely surrounded by broken rock, there are no good campsites. All the lakes permit only flies and lures for fishing, and fires are not allowed above timberline. Good campsites can be established in the protective cover created by the weather-tortured firs. Due to the popularity of American Lakes, you will have little opportunity for solitude. I suggest doing this hike during the week when fewer visitors make the trek to the mountains.

53 Kelly Lake

▶ 7 miles one way   ▶ Moderate

Maps: U.S.G.S. Johnny Moore Mountain, Rawah Lakes

Beginning Elevation: 8,615 feet

Ending Elevation: 10,805 feet

Access Road: Good gravel road last 8.5 miles

Season: Midsummer to fall

Connector Trails: Clear Lake Trail and Hidden Valley Trail

Highlights: Impressive canyon hike to a high cirque lake at the foot of the Rawah Peaks.

To Get There

Take Highway 14 over Cameron Pass to the small town of Gould. From Gould, continue 3 miles west to the KOA campground, located at the State Forest's entrance, and turn right onto CR 41. Pay your $5 daily fee and continue on CR 41 past the North Michigan Reservoir to the end of the road, a distance of 8.5 miles from the KOA. The loop drive at the end of the road is the trailhead, where a restroom and plenty of parking are available. Park and walk past a closed gate down an old logging road.

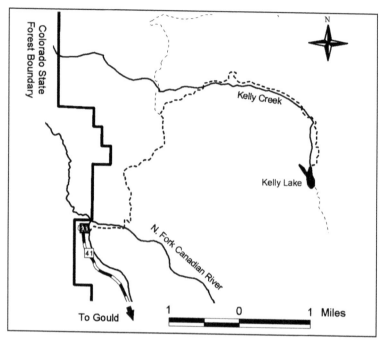

Kelly Lake

The Hike

You will be hiking a dirt road for the first half of the trail, crossing first the South Fork and then the North Fork of the Canadian River at the foot of the hill. A trail fork soon after the North Fork veers off toward the North Fork Canadian yurt. Continue past this turnoff, proceeding through white-barked aspens that dominate the first section of the hike. At a second fork, a sign sits at a funny angle, causing confusion about the direction of the Kelly and Clear Lake Trails. Go left here. (If you cross a large clear-cut area, you've gone the wrong way.) A bit farther along, the Clear Lake Trail shoots off, headed north. Technically, this is the trailhead on most maps.

Beyond this fork, the trail narrows, and the aspens give way to spruces and some enormous, majestic limber pines. The route soon merges

Cairns mark the way to the pass above Kelly Lake

with another logging road for a short distance before veering off into the depths of the forest, so watch closely for signs. After a wide creek crossing over Kelly Creek, you can see the steep canyon walls soaring ahead, and the path begins the ascent, sailing into the elbow of the canyon. Open meadows afford spectacular views of the canyon. A few short sections of trail lead over wooden boardwalk where the route becomes marshy. I rate the difficulty level of the hike to this point as reasonably moderate. However, the last 1.5 miles up to the lake's basin qualifies as strenuous.

Kelly Lake is, by cirque lake standards, good-sized, and snowfields hang off the talus slopes above it. Some of the jagged rock formations enclosing the basin to the east are reminiscent of a lizard's spine, fascinating in the evening light. The lake was named after an old trapper known as Crazy Kelly who lived in Kelly Canyon somewhere below the lake in a cabin he built. Crazy Kelly was fresh off the boat from Ireland when he made North Park his home, and he was very religious, believing his little canyon was heaven. Locals remembered how he lived like a hermit in the mountains for years and occasionally made the trek into Walden for supplies. One year, when he hadn't come around for a while, folks became worried and journeyed up to his cabin to check on him. They found him dead and, not knowing what to do with his body, laid him to rest in his cabin and set the place on fire. No evidence remains of Crazy Kelly's days in Kelly Canyon, but what a spot to call your very own!

Kelly is a popular backpacking and horsepacking destination. However, the basin provides plenty of elbow room and has several established campsites. If you make your own campsite, please leave no trace behind, and be sure to move pack animals frequently to prevent overgrazing.

54 Lake Agnes

▶ 1 mile one way ▶ Moderate

Maps: U.S.G.S. Mount Richthofen

Beginning Elevation: 10,200 feet

Ending Elevation: 10,663 feet

Access Road: Steep rough road last 1.75 miles, but accessible to all cars

Season: Midsummer to fall

Connector Trails: Michigan Ditch Trail

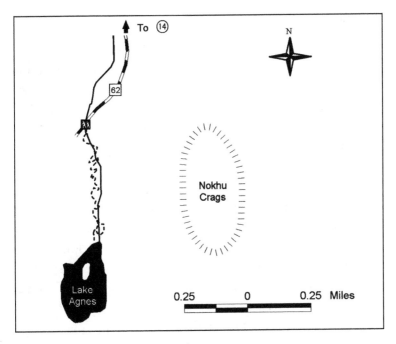

Lake Agnes

Highlights: Glacial lake at foot of Nokhu Crags with a historic cabin at the trailhead, a true North Park special.

To Get There

Drive over Cameron Pass on Highway 14 to the Lake Agnes turnoff. Before entering the State Forest, stop at the entrance station and pay the $4 car fee. At a fork in the road, turn right at the sign pointing to the Lake Agnes trailhead. (Parking is available here if you choose not to drive the steep last 1.75 miles.) You will pass the turnoff to the Crags Campground on the left and the Nokhu Hut turnoff on the right before reaching a large parking area with a historic cabin picturesquely situated against the backdrop of the Nokhu Crags.

The Hike

The cabin at the foot of the Lake Agnes Trail was once part of a boys' camp and is the only cabin remaining of the camp. Unfortunately, after one of the boys drowned in Lake Agnes, the camp closed down. Much to the consternation of many fans, the cabin can no longer be rented for overnight stays due to a deteriorating foundation. A new hut, a little farther down the road but with views just as outstanding, has been opened recently in the old cabin's stead and can be reserved through Never Summer Nordic out of Fort Collins.

A volunteer crew gave the trail from the parking lot to the lake a complete makeover in summer 1999, reinforcing switchbacks and transforming what was once a real lung-burner into a more easily traversable trail. Still, it's a pretty stiff climb into the glacially formed basin at the foot of the Nokhu Crags ("Nokhu" is a shortened version of an Arapaho word pronounced NO-koo and meaning "eagle's nest").

The hike itself is short but direct. Beyond the cabin, you'll notice a large trailhead sign. Follow the path through weathered spruce and firs up a ridge looking down on the Agnes Creek diversion ditch. At the top, the views of the large, deep blue lake exceed expectations. The Nokhu Crags, teetering above the lake, are a northern Colorado icon. Add to this panorama the bonus of an island, velvety with evergreens, in the center of the lake.

Lots of stories circulate about the depth of Lake Agnes, especially among anglers. Some people say no one has found the bottom, even with sounders. Lake Agnes was originally called Island Lake for the island in its center, but it was renamed by John Zimmerman for his youngest daughter, Aggie. Agnes Zimmerman was born December 2, 1880, in Lyons, Nebraska, where her family had to make an emergency stop to bring her into the world on their journey from Minnesota by covered wagon pulled by oxen. Later, the family homesteaded the upper Poudre Canyon area known as Home (now an RV park), where the family ran the Keystone Hotel. After her father's death, Agnes and her sister Eda ran the hotel. Later, after Eda's death, Aggie continued on as the post-mistress. When the state bought the family's property and tore down the majestic old hotel in 1945 with plans for trout-rearing ponds, Aggie moved seasonally between a cabin on Roaring Creek at Kinikinik and a second cabin on Chambers Lake. Agnes Zimmerman died May 15, 1954, in Florence, Colorado.

It is important to remember that park regulations prohibit fires or overnight camping in the Lake Agnes basin. Fishing is by flies and lures only, and there is a two-fish limit. Mountain biking and horseback riding are not allowed beyond the parking area. Lake Agnes is a popular destination, and the State Forest is working to maintain its unique wilderness appeal.

55 Ruby Jewel Lake

▶ **3 miles one way**   ▶ **Moderate**

Maps: U.S.G.S. Clark Peak

Beginning Elevation: 9,800 feet

Ending Elevation: 11,240 feet

Access Road: 4WD required last 2 miles

Season: Midsummer to fall

Connector Trails: Hidden Valley Trail

Highlights: Cirque lake set at the top of a crescent-moon-shaped basin tucked under North Park's highest peak

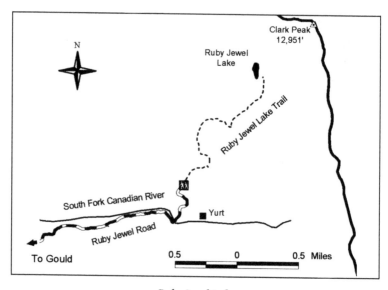

Ruby Jewel Lake

To Get There

Take Highway 14 through Poudre Canyon and over Cameron Pass to the KOA turnoff at the State Forest's entrance just 3 miles north of Gould. Pay your $5 fee at the entrance station to enter the park and continue 4.75 miles on CR 41 past North Michigan Reservoir to the Ruby Jewel turnoff. The last 2 miles of gravel road are rough. You may need to park your car at the green gate and walk the remaining distance. If your vehicle has the clearance, it's possible to drive the entire gravel road to reach the recommended trailhead, a car corral enclosed with buck-and-rail fence, that comes soon after the Ruby Jewel yurt. Beyond the car corral, only 4WD vehicles are recommended.

The Hike

The trail sets off up a 4WD road through fir and lodgepole pine forest with evidence of old sawmills along the way. This stretch of the road is

Ruby Jewel Lake

still open to 4WD vehicles but driving it requires more nerve than most people prefer to muster, and it makes a better walk anyway. As you reach a fork soon after embarking from the trailhead, you may notice some logs defining the site where an old sawmill once stood. Stay left here, but keep a sharp eye for more finds of this sort. The area around Gould was founded by the Michigan River Timber Company back in 1936. Initially the loggers lived in tents but later on built cabins. I spotted four very clear ruins along the trail.

At 1.5 miles, you encounter the official trailhead, and the road narrows to a path. Soon after, you can see to the east the stone buttresses holding up the Ruby Jewel basin. From here, your climb becomes more strenuous as you cross the stream over a footbridge and ascend the ridge. At 2 miles, while climbing through a mature forest of spruce and fir (you couldn't wrap your arms around some of the trees!), you intersect the Hidden Valley cutoff to **Kelly Lake.** Beyond this point, the climb traverses a talus slope along the foot of some stunning rosy-colored cliffs. No fires are allowed beyond timberline, and I recommend finding a campsite among the spruce off to the south (right) where fire rings are already built.

The remaining trek to Ruby Jewel Lake takes you around the curve of the crescent-shaped basin and up to the scree slopes of the cirque basin. The lake is small, nestled into a pocket of rock, and has not been stocked in years, so fishing is poor. The east side has sandbars that create a picturesque effect in the right light. With only a few scraggly subalpine firs along one tip, Ruby Jewel is a lake of extremes in terms of wind and weather.

To make the trek to the top of North Park's highest summit, locate the zigzag line up the south ridge of the basin. Clark Peak looms above, safeguarded on two sides by lower peaks, Sickle Peak to the north, Pipit Peak to the south, all three visible from the basin. The trail is nonexistent, and there are no cairns beyond the ridge, but the way is clear. Hike up the flank of Pipit Peak, then down the other side to the long, cliff-edged trail toward the summit of Clark Peak. Views into the Rawah Wilderness are astonishing from up here. Many people argue about whether Clark Peak was named for J. Max Clark, a founding member of Union Colony (Greeley), or Rufus B. (Potato) Clark, who introduced the potato to Colorado fields. In a string of mountains named after birds (Chickadee, Pipit, Grosbeak, Raven, etc.), isn't it possible the peak is named not for a man but for a bird—the Clark's Nutcracker perhaps?

NEVER SUMMER WILDERNESS AREA

A small tract of land nestled into a corner of North Park, the Never Summer Wilderness of the Routt National Forest is abutted on its eastern boundary by the ragged high country of Rocky Mountain National Park. It was named after the Arapaho word for the area—ni-chebe-chii ("never no summer")—by the naming party of 1914. This is rugged, undiscovered country. Most of its trails have few or no designated campsites and require meticulous "leave no trace" tactics. Most of the trailheads into the area are remote, and access roads are usually rough. The trail described here for **Baker Pass** via the South Fork Trail is one of the more accessible and least strenuous trails into the area and can be used for more extensive explorations. Backcountry permits are not required unless you intend to continue on into Rocky Mountain National Park. For more information, contact the Routt National Forest Office in Walden at (970) 723-8402.

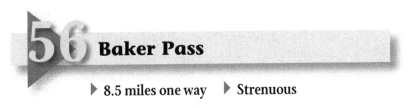

56 Baker Pass

▶ 8.5 miles one way ▶ Strenuous

Maps: U.S.G.S. Mount Richthofen
Beginning Elevation: 9,320 feet
Ending Elevation: 11,253 feet
Access Road: Medium-grade gravel road last 6 miles
Season: Midsummer to fall

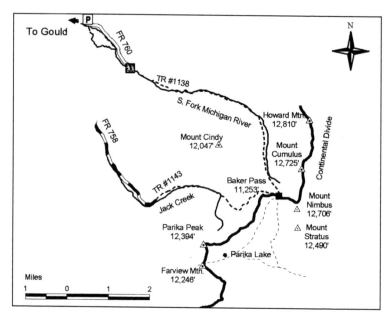

Baker Pass

Connector Trails: Jack Creek Trail #1143, Never Summer Trail #1141

Highlights: This long hike takes you along a wide stream into a little-known wilderness area to a mountain pass on the Continental Divide for views into Rocky Mountain National Park.

To Get There

From Cameron Pass, drive east to the small town of Gould and turn left (south) on FR 740, proceeding about 5 miles past Aspen and Pines Campgrounds to a three-way fork. Take the middle fork, FR 760. After about 1.5 miles, this road becomes an impassable, rutted 4WD road with very few places to park or turn around. I recommend parking in the space available where a road sign designates 4WD begins, then walking the final 2 miles to the trailhead.

Mount Nimbus soars above Baker Pass

The Hike

From the "4WD Road Ahead" sign, walk up the narrow track about 1 mile to a fork in the road and go left, straight up a rocky hill. A wooden sign points in the direction of the South Fork Trail #1138, the trail you want. From here, the trail loses even the most adventurous 4WD vehicles and narrows to a track used by all-terrain vehicles (ATVs). This section offers a pleasant campsite, and even the isolated trailhead would make a fine spot, although there are no fire rings. About 0.5 mile past it, you enter the Never Summer Wilderness. Although the South Fork Trail shows the Never Summer area in a gentle light, this is rough, challenging country, most of it soaring well above timberline. Beyond the trailhead, the trail becomes a foot path closed to mechanized travel, following alongside the wide, willowy South Fork of the Michigan River, a major tributary of the North Platte River. The stream is a destination for many anglers and is a good place to spot moose that graze on the willow bushes along the river. This is a place with few human disturbances and a good opportunity to practice quiet, unobtrusive backcountry ethics. Views of the gorge walls and the lower flank of Mount Cindy to the south are superb.

As the trail continues at an easy climb alongside the creek, crossing many small streamlets, be prepared to muck across some marshy sections. When necessary, follow trail posts. Soon you'll see ahead the red Mount Cumulus and behind it the craggy, gothic-looking Mount Nimbus. These are two mountains in a string of them named for cloud formations, a reminder of the turbulent weather common to the high country. Both mountains lie just inside Rocky Mountain National Park. Their redness can be attributed to the volcanic past of the Never Summer Range.

At the end of another broad park, trail posts lead across the often deep creek. No footbridge is provided here. You will begin climbing at an increasingly strenuous incline through lovely forest. Follow rock cairns and trail posts up into alpine meadows for views back onto the creek drainage behind you. Above timberline, the intensity of the pink-hued mountaintops fills your view as you near the pass. This last stretch is a real challenge but well worth the effort when you reach the saddle located between Mount Nimbus and an unnamed peak to the west. From here, you can identify Parika and Farview Peaks to the south. The Jack Creek Trail #1143 ascends the unnamed summit to the west; the Never Summer Trail #1141 takes off a short distance below the north side of the pass, headed cross-country to Seven Utes Mountain. Meanwhile, yet another trail follows rock cairns down into Baker Gulch and up a steep draw to Parika Lake, another 3.5 miles farther. Baker Pass straddles the Continental Divide and is also the county line between Jackson and Grand Counties.

ROUTT NATIONAL FOREST

Even outside its wilderness areas, the Routt National Forest offers an abundance of hiking destinations that give you a genuine sense of getting off the beaten path. The Routt National Forest surrounds the valley of North Park on three sides, skirting the Zirkel and Never Summer Wildernesses. You won't be battling the crowds at the trailheads listed here. However, you can expect to share the trail with mountain bikes and all-terrain vehicles (ATVs), as these trails are open to motorized traffic. The Routt National Forest does not enforce a leash law but does require that all pets be under immediate verbal command. For more information, contact the Routt National Forest Office at (970) 723-8204.

57 Arapaho Ridge Trail #1135

▶ **10 miles one way** ▶ **Strenuous**

Maps: U.S.G.S. Buffalo Peak, Hyannis Peak, Rand

Beginning Elevation: 9,800 feet

Ending Elevation: 9,600 feet

Access Road: Medium-grade gravel road last 1.75 miles

Season: Midsummer to fall

Connector Trails: Arapaho Creek Trail #1187 to Sheep Mountain. The Arapaho Ridge Trail is 10 miles long with a trailhead at each end.

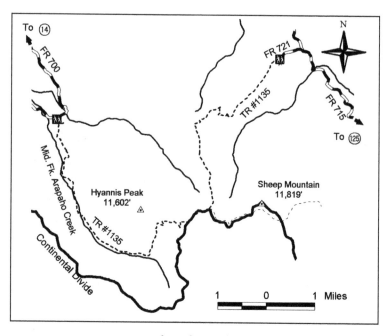

Arapaho Ridge Trail #1135

Highlights: Views of North Park and the Never Summer Range from the top of this alpine ridge are unbeatable.

To Get There

From Fort Collins, take Highway 14 100 miles to Walden and continue west out of town to the junction of Highway 125 and 14 and go straight on Highway 125 to Rand, 21 miles from Walden. Four miles past Rand, after entering the Routt National Forest, turn right onto the Willow Creek Road (FR 106). Then turn right again on FR 715, continuing to the FR 721 turnoff where you turn left (a sign has been posted here to the Grassy Run trailhead). Proceed 1.75 miles on FR 721 to its dead-end at a clear-cut area where the trailhead is located. There are ample camping opportunities along the Willow Creek Road and FR 721.

An unusual rock face visible from the Arapaho Ridge Trail

The Hike

You can make the Arapaho Ridge Trail a good two-car shuttle back-packing destination by leaving a second vehicle at the Hyannis Peak trailhead at the other end, accessed off Highway 14 between Walden and Rabbit Ears Pass by taking CR 11 past Seymour Lake until it turns into FR 700. Just past Bundy Park, a trailhead and limited parking provide access to the Arapaho Ridge Trail's west end. However, keep in mind that much of the middle section of the trail traverses alpine country and offers little by way of campsites. The best camping opportunities are at the lower elevations along the Middle Fork of the Arapaho Creek some 7 miles from the Grassy Run trailhead, closer to the west trailhead. Be prepared for lots of creek wading and mosquitoes along the stream.

Currently, the Arapaho Ridge Trail is open to motorbikes, although officials are considering whether to close the trail to motorized use. Most motorized traffic accesses the area by way of the Grassy Run trailhead rather than by the west trailhead. For more information on the status of the trail, contact the Routt National Forest Office in Walden.

The trail climbs straight up from the trailhead, following an old road that is wide and washed out but easy to navigate. The lower sections of the trail take you through immature stands of lodgepole pine, entering fir and spruce forest as it climbs in elevation. As you round the east flank of the ridge, views soon open up. Watch for a beautiful white rock face (more noticeable on the return trip) behind you. You can see Sheep Mountain with its rocky slopes across a draw. The wildflowers taking advantage of the sunlight on these steep slopes are a riot of color during July and early August.

Soon the trail reaches timberline and tops out at 11,450 feet with views of the full length and majesty of Arapaho Ridge cutting a south-easterly course. Red-knobbed Hyannis Peak can be seen to the southwest as the trail follows the spine of the ridge to drop off just below Hyannis Peak into the lush Middle Fork of Arapaho Creek drainage. At a switchback below the peak, it is possible to ascend the steep summit off-trail. It's an extra 1 mile to the top.

A 3-mile stretch of the Arapaho Ridge Trail traverses country well above timberline, and trekkers must be careful not to be caught up here when the inevitable afternoon lightning storms descend. About midway along the trail, you will intersect the Arapaho Creek Trail, a hiker-made side trail for those interested in summiting Sheep Mountain. Watch for five stone circles (or tepee rings, although their function is unknown) located near the north end of the ridge soon after you reach the top. After the Meeker massacre of 1879, some Ute bands sought shelter in this vicinity and were blamed for a forest fire nearby; the scars are still visible to the west. Could the stone circles have been fire rings used as signals to other bands? No one knows.

58 Teller City

▸ 0.75-mile loop ▸ Easy

Maps: U.S.G.S. Jack Creek

Elevation: 9,291 feet

Access Road: Access #1 is good gravel road last 7 miles; Access #2 requires high-clearance vehicle last 4 miles.

Season: Midsummer to fall

Connector Trails: None

Highlights: This one-of-a-kind loop walk takes you through the streets of a ghost town located in a beautiful mountain hollow with opportunities for further explorations.

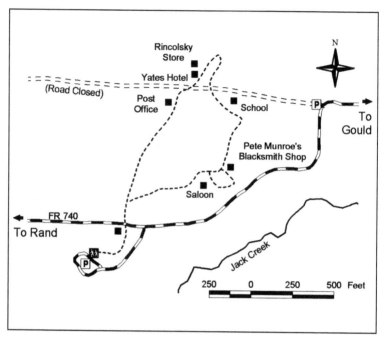

Teller City

To Get There

Access #1: Take Highway 14 to Walden and out of town west on Highway 125 south to Rand. After reaching Rand at 21 miles, continue south on Highway 125 another 5 miles to FR 740 and follow signs 7 miles to Teller City. Proceed 1 mile past a "Teller City Day Use Area" sign, and watch for a turnoff on the right, just after a renovated cabin. Drive in to a parking area loop and park.

Access #2: Take Highway 14 over Cameron Pass to the town of Gould and head west on FR 740 past Aspen and Pines Campgrounds. At a four-way junction in the road, follow a sign to Teller City, staying right on FR 740 over Calamity Pass, a classic 4WD road—rutted, winding, steep, and narrow. Near the bottom of the pass, take a minute to read a sign posted at a fence about Teller City's history, then continue past one of the better-preserved cabins to the parking area, located just behind a renovated cabin. No restrooms are available at the trailhead.

The Hike

Teller City was the first town in North Park, a boom town that sprang up in 1879 when Jack Bishop discovered silver along Jack Creek (named after him), about 3.5 miles upstream from the town's location. In the town's heyday, 1,300 people lived here, mostly young men in search of fortune. (Women were so scarce, the boys practiced "heifer branding" at dances in which some of them wore a handkerchief on their arm and took the ladies' part.) But Teller City also boasted a school, post office, newspaper, blacksmith, two doctors and twenty-seven saloons! A forty-room hotel was built by the LaFaevre brothers and called the Yates House. At that time, North Park was part of Grand County, and carriers on snowshoe brought mail over Bowen Pass to Grand Lake through high country notorious for its avalanches. By 1883, the mines had closed for lack of capital to fund the process of reducing silver ore to bullion. People left so quickly that dirty dishes were left on the tables, and clothes still hung in the closets. Many of these items can be seen at Walden's Pioneer Museum.

Locate a packed gravel path lined with stones headed through the trees toward the renovated cabin. A volunteer trail crew recently built the path as part of a trail project. The trail is handicapped-accessible but somewhat bumpy where moose and cattle have wandered through. In the future, expect to find informational displays complete with old photos near the new cabin.

Continue up the path and across the road through a gap in a buck-and-rail fence and stay straight at a fork. The first few structures you'll see were the homes of several citizens who lived on what would have been Main Street. Most are two-room dirt-floor cabins. People had to hang

The renovated cabin at Teller City

newspapers on the walls against the winter draft. Follow the trail as it crosses an abandoned road. A bench sits overlooking what is left of the Yates House, which is nothing but the outline of the foundation. Much of Teller City was "salvaged," cabins moved piecemeal or whole into Rand, some by their former owners (today it is illegal to remove anything from a historic site). The Rincolsky Store sits just to the north.

Once you've recrossed the old access road, a second log bench marks a side loop past three more cabins; one of them must be Pete Munroe's old blacksmith shop. The trail returns to the parking area the way it came. Further exploration off-trail from the 230 confirmed cabin ruins is worth the effort. Some sources say a graveyard with five or six unmarked mounds can be found nearby. Teller City is a day-use area only. Plenty of camping is available outside the 1-mile radius of the ghost town (in the suburbs, so to speak).

Zirkel Wilderness

Named after a petrologist who invented a new rock-identification technique and who lived in a rustic cabin in one of the many gorges cutting off the Continental Divide, the Zirkel Wilderness has become one of Colorado's most beloved wilderness destinations. The Zirkel Wilderness, accessed from Walden about 100 miles from Fort Collins, includes a large tract of unspoiled land straddling the Continental Divide along the Park Range. The Continental Divide Trail, or the Wyoming Trail #1101, skitters down the spine of the wilderness area. Canyons plunge off the Divide feeding glacially formed moraines and an almost infinite number of cirque lakes waiting to be discovered, both on and off trail. One stretch of the Continental Divide running through the Zirkel Wilderness gets the most precipitation of anywhere in the state (mostly in the form of snow), and this moisture is necessary because the Zirkel Wilderness serves as the headwaters of the North Platte River to the east and the Yampa River to the west. This is wet country, and both day hikers and backpackers should come expecting afternoon thunderstorms during the summer months. Trails lead on and off the Continental Divide, making for good loop trips or two-car shuttles that might include one of the many trailheads to the west, accessible from the Steamboat Springs side of the Zirkel Wilderness. For more information, contact the Routt National Forest Office in Walden at (970) 723-8204.

Bear Lakes/Ute Pass Trail #1180

▶ 5.5 miles to Bear Lakes ▶ Strenuous
5.25 miles to Ute Pass

Maps: U.S.G.S. Boettcher Lake, Mount Zirkel, Pitchpine Mountain

Beginning Elevation: 8,860 feet

Ending Elevation: 11,000 feet

Access Road: Good gravel road, all cars

Season: Midsummer to fall

Connector Trails: Ute Creek Trail #1128, Gold Creek Lake Trail #1150.

Highlights: Fascinating rock formations in a large canyon with views, hidden lakes, and a historical passage over the Continental Divide.

To Get There

Take Highway 14 to Walden and continue out of town west on Highway 14/125 to CR 12W toward Lake John. At the Y junction with CR 18, turn right on CR 12W. Follow the road as it turns to gravel, bypassing CR 7. The road crosses the Lone Pine Ranch, enters Routt National Forest, and becomes FR 640. The first trailhead encountered will be on the left, the Grizzly-Helena Trail headed south. The second trailhead is the Grizzly-Helena Trail headed north and is the access trail to the Bear Lakes/Ute Pass Trail #1180. If you reach the end of the road at a third trailhead, the Lone Pine Trail to **Lakes Katherine** and **Bighorn,** you've gone too far. No parking area is provided for the Grizzly-Helena trailhead north. Park on the side of the road and walk up the trail beyond the sign.

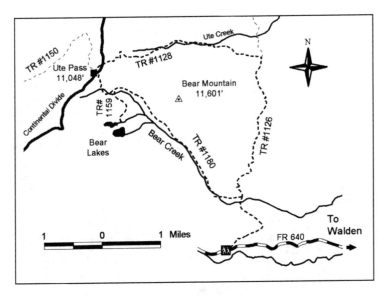

Bear Lakes/Ute Pass Trail #1180

The Hike

The trail begins ascending through vibrant aspen forest, muddy most times of year, then enters Engelmann spruce forest as it reaches more level terrain. After crossing Bear Creek, you meet a sign posted to Ute Pass at 1.5 miles. This is also the trail junction to Bear Lakes. If you choose to make a loop of the hike, the return trail #1128 intersects the Grizzly-Helena Trail 2 miles farther north. After heading west, the trail reaches lusher spruce and subalpine forest, hugging the creek as it steadily climbs. At 2 miles, a well-preserved old cabin located at the foot of a gorgeous orange rock face is all that's left of an old mine. You can see where the mining occurred by walking up the trail around the back side of the rock and looking up the talus slope to see an orange streak near the place of excavation. The Bear Creek canyon soon grows wide with sweeping views from wildflower meadows. The canyon shows off an orange cliff face, fading to a pink in the upper reaches.

A creek crossing at Bear Lakes

Beyond these meadows, the trail is an increasingly strenuous climb, stair-stepping up until you seem almost at eye level with timberline. The trail to Bear Lakes is unsigned. Just as the trail makes a switchback at 4.75 miles, notice a cairn (rock pile) on the left leading down into the deep, heavily wooded basin below. The trail appears neglected and grown over, but if you look down at the line of trees, you'll see a second cairn. You'll know you've gone one switchback too many if you pass the small pond on the left just before the climb to the pass.

As you embark on the trail into Bear Lakes, another 0.75 mile off the main track, watch for cairns to lead you across the creek, which creates a soggy marsh where a definite trail easily becomes overgrown. The hike down into the basin is steep and rocky, but the three lakes are just reward, hidden as they are among the trees and rocks. Although native and brown trout reportedly are found in these lakes, I saw few fish rising during an early August visit, and neighboring anglers were glum. You can find campsites on the east end of the largest lake and on the strip of high ground between the large and the midsized lakes.

It is another 0.5 mile from the cairn marking the Bear Lakes Trail junction up to the top of Ute Pass on the Continental Divide, the pass historically used by the Yampa Ute bands to access North Park. (A second Ute Pass crosses the Medicine Bow Range almost directly across the other side of North Park.) It's a difficult but worthwhile ascent to the saddle with views of the Bear Creek gorge behind you. To access Ute Creek and make a loop hike, catch Trail #1128 at the pass heading north and down a neighboring draw.

Big Creek Falls Trail #1125

▶ 1.5 miles one way ▶ Moderate

Maps: U.S.G.S. Pearl, Davis Peak

Beginning Elevation: 9,020 feet

Ending Elevation: 9,160 feet

Access Road: Good gravel road last 22 miles

Season: Midsummer through fall

Connector Trails: Red Elephant Nature Trail; **Seven Lakes Trail #1125** continues to Seven Lakes.

Highlights: A forest of great diversity, views of Upper Big Creek Lake, and opportunities for wildlife viewing make North Park's most famous waterfall well worth a visit.

To Get There

Take Highway 14 to Walden and drive north on Highway 125 to Cowdrey. At the Cowdrey Store, turn left on CR 6W. The road turns to gravel after a few miles, curving around Independence Mountain. Continue on CR 6W to the sign to Big Creek Lake just before the ghost town of Pearl. CR 6W turns into FR 600 at the Routt National Forest boundary. The drive from Cowdrey to the trailhead is about 22 miles, most of it gravel. At Big Creek Lake, go straight at the fork, following signs to the trailhead. The parking lot, on the left past the campground, provides restrooms and brochures.

The Hike

At the trailhead, help yourself to a Red Elephant Nature Trail guide, using it on the first mile of your hike to identify plants and points of

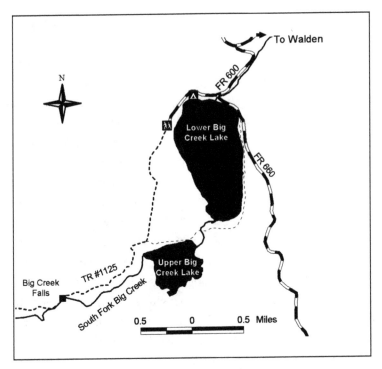

Big Creek Falls Trail #1125

interest. Red Elephant is the prominent reddish mountain visible above Big Creek Lake, the second-largest natural lake in Colorado. Also notice the information board discussing the 1997 blowdown in the Zirkel Wilderness Area. Although I saw no sign of uprooted trees on my trip, it's interesting to read about the event. The blowdown ravaged thousands of acres of forest primarily on the west side of the Divide.

The trail into Big Creek Falls is very popular because of its proximity to Big Creek Lake and its use as an access to Upper Big Creek Lake, so don't expect much solitude unless you hike midweek or in the autumn, a beautiful time to walk along a path strewn with gold and red aspen leaves. The lodgepole pine forest flourishes along a marshy area, which you cross by way of a wooden boardwalk. (Because of the marsh, horse travel is not recommended.

The trail forks at 0.75 mile. To continue the Red Elephant Nature Trail or to reach the shore of Upper Big Creek Lake, go left. To walk on to Big Creek Falls, stay right. After the fork, the forest changes to Engelmann spruce mixed with subalpine fir and aspen. Many mixtures of wildflowers, such as alpine aster, pussytoes, and Indian paintbrush, grow along this stretch of trail. At the rocky outcropping looking over Upper Big Creek Lake, stop and watch for osprey, a bird of prey introduced to North Park, diving for fish below. Two nests have been built for the birds on the lake. If you have binoculars, one nest is visible (but not approachable) from the trail. It's a real treat if you can spy a parent babysitting from the top of a dead tree nearby. These birds were recently on the endangered species list, and North Park is happy to make them welcome.

As you continue up the trail, you'll soon hear the falls through the trees below. To see Big Creek Falls in its glory, plan an early trip during summer runoff. The falls drop from a height of about 30 feet, pooling below under the dark, chilly forest. A path can take you above the falls to the rock platform it flows over. A beautiful place, a North Park pride and joy.

Trail #1125 continues to Seven Lakes, accessing a large basin at the foot of Red Elephant Mountain.

Bighorn Lake Trail #1040

▶ **13.5 miles one way**   ▶ **Strenuous**

Maps: U.S.G.S. Pitchpine, Mount Ethel, Mount Zirkel

Beginning Elevation: 8,900 feet

Ending Elevation: 10,400 feet

Access Road: Good gravel road

Season: Midsummer to fall

Connector Trails: Wyoming Trail #1101

Highlights: A glacially formed and very deep cirque lake within a
   day's hike into the beautiful Zirkel Wilderness with views of a
   majestic canyon.

To Get There

   Take Highway 14 to Walden and head west out of town on Highway
14/125 to CR 12W, the Lake John turnoff. Continue on CR 12W as it
veers north at an intersection with CR 18. At a T in the road, turn left,
sticking with CR 12W, following a "National Forest Access" sign. The
road crosses the Lone Pine Ranch for quite a distance, then bumps over
a cattle guard and enters national forest, becoming FR 640 at the boundary. You will pass two other trailheads (Grizzly-Helena Trail North and
South) before reaching the end of the road and the Lone Pine trailhead
to Bighorn Lake and the **Lake Katherine Trail.** There are several good
campsites along FR 640 as well as one or two sites without much privacy
at the trailhead.

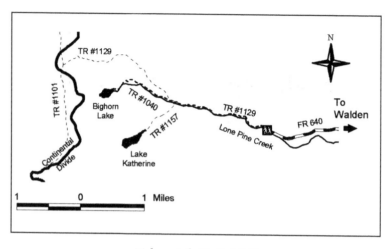

Bighorn Lake Trail #1040

The Hike

From the parking area, walk beyond the trailhead sign, remembering to sign the register for the sake of posterity and safety. Proceed up the Lone Pine Trail #1129 where you soon cross a clattery boardwalk that serves to protect the willowy marshland underfoot. The wet meadows last only a few yards before the trail meanders its way into the pleasant darkness of the spruce and fir forest that will dominate your upcoming hike. At 0.5 mile, the path reaches the Zirkel Wilderness boundary where no motorized vehicles, including mountain bikes, are allowed. Be aware that at certain times of year, you may encounter cattle grazing on public lands, including wilderness areas.

The first 1.5 miles are moderately strenuous as the path wanders within an audible distance of Lone Pine Creek. At a second section of boardwalk, 1 mile up the trail, the forest opens up to views of the canyon, a vista made possible by an old avalanche path. Neighboring **Red Canyon** with its cliffs of red rock might be more gothic, but Lone Pine

A morning fog lifts over Bighorn Lake

Canyon has a certain loveliness of its own. At 1.5 miles, Lone Pine Trail forks. The path up to the Continental Divide (still called the Lone Pine Trail) steers right, intersecting the Wyoming Trail #1101 at 2.5 miles farther. Immediately after, you'll reach a Y at the creek. Left takes you to Lake Katherine, right to Bighorn Lake.

Your climb becomes increasingly strenuous as the trail continues up through old-growth fir and spruce forest before reaching the foot of the plateau upon which Bighorn Lake and its two companion lakes lie. The steep climb is rocky and somewhat treacherous, but you'll be rewarded as you approach the lakes through the wet undergrowth and reach Bighorn's outlet pond. Even in early July, this area can be banked in snow. Stick with the creek and you'll reach your destination. Bighorn Lake is deep and fairly fishable (unlike Lake Katherine) with large Mackinaw trout hiding out at depths of more than 115 feet. Particularly nice fishing can be had in the outlet stream between Bighorn Lake proper and the pond below. More delightful campsites are available at Bighorn Lake in either direction from the footbridge for those willing to search a bit along the higher ridges, and plenty of fire rings already exist. Bighorn Lake is one of North Park's most popular destinations for a reason—it's a magical place and therefore a challenge to keep that way. Please pack out anything you pack in.

Lake Katherine Trail #1157

▶ **3.5 miles one way**   ▶ **Strenuous**

Maps: U.S.G.S. Pitchpine, Mount Ethel, Mount Zirkel

Beginning Elevation: 8,900 feet

Ending Elevation: 10,400 feet

Access Road: Good gravel road

Season: Midsummer to fall

Connector Trails: Wyoming Trail #1101

Highlights: A glacially formed cirque lake within a day's hike into the beautiful Zirkel Wilderness with views of a majestic canyon and a waterfall.

To Get There

Take Highway 14 to Walden and head west out of town on Highway 14/125 to CR 12W, the Lake John turnoff. Continue on CR 12W

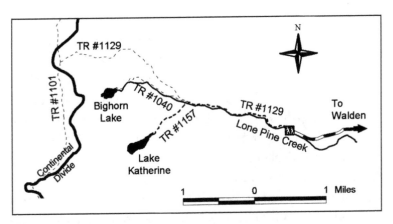

Lake Katherine Trail #1157

as it veers north at an intersection with CR 18. At a T in the road, turn left, sticking with CR 12W as it crosses private property. The road enters national forest, becoming FR 640 at the boundary. You will pass two other trailheads (Grizzly-Helena Trail North and South) before reaching the end of the road and the Lone Pine trailhead. There are several good campsites along FR 640 as well as one or two sites without much privacy at the trailhead.

The Hike

From the parking area, walk beyond the trailhead sign, remembering to sign the register for the sake of posterity and safety. Proceed up the Lone Pine Trail #1129 where you very soon cross a clattery boardwalk that serves to protect the willowy marshland underfoot. After the wet meadows, the trail meanders its way into the pleasant darkness of the spruce and fir forest that will dominate your upcoming hike. At 0.5 mile, the path reaches the Zirkel Wilderness boundary where no motorized vehicles, including mountain bikes, are allowed. Be aware that at certain times of year, you may encounter cattle grazing on public lands, including wilderness areas.

The first 1.5 miles are moderately strenuous as the path wanders within an audible distance of Lone Pine Creek. At a second section of boardwalk, 1 mile up the trail, the forest opens up to views of the canyon, a vista made possible by an old avalanche path. At 1.5 miles, Lone Pine Trail forks. The path up to the Continental Divide (still called the Lone Pine Trail) steers right, intersecting the Wyoming Trail #1101 at 2.5 miles farther up the draw. Immediately after, you'll reach a Y. Here, fording the creek may be a difficult endeavor during runoff. Left takes you to Lake Katherine, right to Bighorn Lake. The best spot to cross the creek if water is high is upstream a stretch, over a large log.

After the juncture, the way becomes increasingly strenuous, eventually resorting to switchbacks. At 2 miles, watch for a couple of overlooks where you can watch the creek as it tumbles out of the basin above. The best time of year to see the Lake Katherine falls is June or July, but also be prepared for snow obscuring the trail. Also from this lookout are superb views of the canyon itself. At 2.5 miles, the path reaches the lovely Lake Katherine, an unusually emerald lake. The startling color is caused by the suspension of glacial dust, or rock flour, in the water. The lake is horseshoe-shaped with a second arm of it bending out of view.

Two overused campsites exist on the hump of the horseshoe, but I suggest finding a place farther from the lake or camping at Bighorn Lake where there are more appropriate campsites in greater numbers. (The rule for camping distance from water is 40 paces, or 100 yards.)

At a rock bridge (an old masonry dam built long ago to increase the lake's storage capacity) you can look across the stream to find an old cabin still partly standing. Like many cirque lakes, much of the lake is surrounded by scree slopes that can be tricky and dangerous footing. Unlike Bighorn Lake, Lake Katherine is not much of a fishing lake. However, it is still a popular hiking destination, and you shouldn't expect much opportunity for solitude.

Rainbow Lakes Trail #1130

▶ 3.75 miles one way ▶ Moderate

Maps: U.S.G.S. Pitchpine Mountain, Mount Ethel

Beginning Elevation: 8,760 feet

Ending Elevation: 9,854 feet

Access Road: Medium-grade gravel road last 2 miles

Season: Midsummer to fall

Connector Trails: Trail #1130 continues to Slide, Upper Slide, and Roxy Ann Lake as well as to the **Wyoming Trail #1101.** Also accesses the Grizzly-Helena Trail.

Highlights: The trail meanders through lovely mixed conifer and aspen forest up to the largest lake in the Zirkel Wilderness with two small lakes below it and a wild waterfall above and opportunities for longer excursions.

To Get There

Take Highway 14 to Walden and head out of town west on Highway 125/14, veering right onto CR 12W and following a sign toward Lake John. Stay straight on CR 18 when CR 12W curves right. At a Y in the road, go left on CR 5. At this point, the road turns to gravel and later becomes CR 22 (CR 5 veers away to the left). Stay right at an unnumbered road fork; the one on the left is a ranch driveway. The road continues past several cabins and a rock with the word "slow" on it in blue spray paint. This is a private road accessing summer homes, and it becomes very winding and rocky. After a few miles of zigzagging through private property, you'll see a Forest Service sign ahead and a large parking area. There is little camping along CR 22.

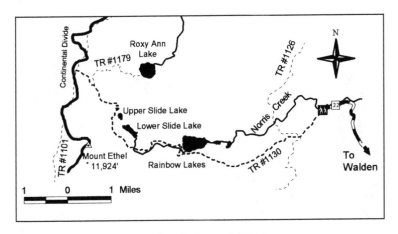

Rainbow Lakes trail #1130

The Hike

The Rainbow Lakes Trail is a popular backpacking route with little opportunity for solitude unless your sights are set on the Continental Divide or possibly Slide, Upper Slide, and Roxy Ann Lake. The trail begins climbing immediately. At 1 mile, the Rainbow Lakes Trail intersects the Grizzly-Helena Trail, a 38-mile connector route open to motorized use. Beyond this junction, you enter the Zirkel Wilderness, open to foot traffic only. Continue straight here toward Rainbow Lakes. Climbing along the ridge above the draw leading into Rainbow Lakes gives you majestic views of North Park. At 3 miles, the trail meets Norris Creek, easily crossed by a log footbridge. After the creek, the climb becomes briefly more strenuous, then drops. You'll see Middle Rainbow Lake through the trees. Rainbow Lake itself lies above. The two are connected by a rollicking stream. A third lake, Lower Rainbow Lake, is accessed below Middle Rainbow by a patchy path formed by anglers, and this lake has some good fishing. Snow often remains in deep banks along the south shores of Rainbow Lake well into the summer. Notice the pink tint on the snow. This is a high mountain algae that grows on snow and

The waterfalls below Rainbow Lakes

reportedly tastes like watermelon. (There's no guarantee of its effect on the digestion, however.)

The trail continues along the south shore, accessing campsites, some of which are closed due to resource damage. To hike up to Slide Lakes, follow this trail around the western tip of Rainbow Lakes to the wide stream, crossed by way of a large log. You'll see and hear white raging falls ahead. The 2-mile trail to Slide Lakes climbs right next to the roaring water. No official trail accesses Lower Slide Lake. To reach it, follow the creek draining it up to where it flows over a unique rock wash, polished smooth by the flowing water. (You can identify the rock creek bed from the trail.) Farther up Trail #1130 is a posted trail that accesses Upper Slide Lake. Both are moderately popular. Almost at the foot of the Continental Divide, a 1.5-mile side trail accesses Roxy Ann Lake by way of a steep rocky descent. Roxy Ann Lake provides the headwaters of the Roaring Fork, a large tributary of the North Platte River that carves through **Red Canyon.** Total distance from the Rainbow Lakes trailhead to the Continental Divide is 8.25 miles, and here you access the Wyoming Trail #1101 headed south to Luna Lake or north to Red Canyon.

64. Red Canyon Trail #1131 to Lost Ranger Peak

▶ **7.75 miles one way** ▶ **Strenuous**

Maps: U.S.G.S. Pitchpine Mountain, Mount Ethel

Beginning Elevation: 8,511 feet

Ending Elevation: 11,932 feet

Access Road: Rough 4WD road last 2 miles

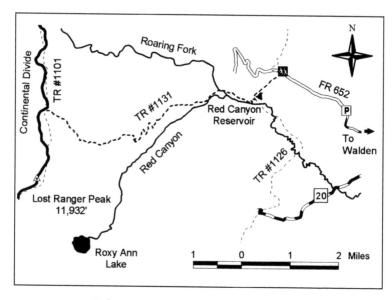

Red Canyon Trail #1131 to Lost Ranger Peak

Distance One Way: 7.75 miles

Difficulty: Strenuous

Season: Midsummer through fall

Connector Trails: Grizzly-Helena Trail #1126, Wyoming Trail #1101

Highlights: Magical canyon experience offering ferny aspen forest, waterfalls, and 360-degree views from the top.

To Get There

Take Highway 14 to Walden and continue west on Highway 125/14. Go right on CR 12W at the Lake John turnoff just outside of town. Soon, CR 12W curves north. Stay straight on CR 18. At a Y, turn right on CR 5, which becomes CR 20 after passing Delaney Butte Lakes. At some large oil tanks 15 miles from Walden, turn right onto a gravel track, CR 652. Soon the road forks; continue left on CR 652, turning

View of Red Canyon from Lost Ranger Peak

left. Immediately, you'll reach a state trust sign. The road becomes increasingly rocky and washed-out from here, and you'll need 4WD and nerves of steel as the road climbs. A parking area is provided past the state trust boundary, and there is more parking farther along for those with low-clearance vehicles (in which case, add 3 miles to the total hiking distance). The road dead-ends at the trailhead overlooking an eye-popping view of Red Canyon. Park here. The last 0.5 mile of the road penetrates the outer edge of the 2001 burn.

The Hike

In the late summer of 2001, a large swath of Red Canyon burned. You will see some of the burn in the drive up, but you can expect to see more of the burn and its results on the first 2 miles of the Red Canyon Trail. Where the trail once descended through man-high cow parsnip and fern, you will now see new plant life flourishing, in an order that builds in complexity and vitality as the years pass. Wilderness trail crews worked on the trail in 2006 to clear any dangerous trees from the trailside, and you can confidently explore the revival of a forest after a fire along the first brief section of this trip.

The hike down is steep, and the climb out a real killer. At the mouth of the canyon lies a pond, where signs warn trespassers to beware of private property. Look but don't touch. The trail then climbs into the rocks and intersects the Grizzly-Helena Trail. By following the Grizzly-Helena Trail a short distance south, it is possible to view the Red Canyon waterfall. The Roaring Fork flows smoothly alongside as the trail enters the Zirkel Wilderness. You will have to cross the creek once before beginning to climb high along the wall of the towering canyon. At about 2.5 miles, the trail reaches a secluded sagebrush meadow, colorful with lupine, Indian paintbrush, wild geranium, and other wild flowers. This is a perfect place to conclude a day hike into Red Canyon. An old prospector's cabin sits across the creek, and the views of the canyon walls from this spot are unrivaled. Red Canyon's unusual burnished look is attributable to fountain sandstone.

Beyond this point, the burn is less noticeable. The trail begins to climb in earnest, scaling the wall of the canyon toward a rocky ridge, leaving behind the creek that curves south to drain Roxy Ann Lake (accessible from the **Rainbow Lakes Trail**). The trail crosses two major creeks, the second a torrent. After this waterfall, the trail reaches more switchbacks, then levels off. A large campsite is available amid the old-growth forest. It is the only permanent campsite in Red Canyon. Wouldn't it be nice to keep it that way? If you choose to make your own campsite, please leave no trace.

Soon you encounter the alpine meadows of the Continental Divide as you make a broad loop around the knob of Lost Ranger Peak. The trail disappears across these boggy parks, and you'll need to follow rock cairns. They are easy to follow in all but one spot. Watch for posts above on the mountainside, and from there the trail again becomes visible, with a sign posted to identify the Wyoming Trail that climbs directly over Lost Ranger Peak to access Luna Lake and Buffalo Pass. The summit is a (relatively) gentle wildflower-speckled climb, affording 360-degree views of Ute Pass and Mount Zirkel to the north, the Dome to the southwest, Hahns Peak and Wolverine basin and its lakes to the west, and, best of all, Red Canyon to the east—majestic, mystical, wild.

Seven Lakes Trail #1125

▶ **7 miles one way**   ▶ **Moderate**

Maps: U.S.G.S. Pearl, Davis Peak

Beginning Elevation: 9,020 feet

Ending Elevation: 11,422 feet

Access Road: Good gravel road last 22 miles

Season: Midsummer through fall

Connector Trails: Beaver Creek Trail #1124, Encampment Meadows Trail #1152, and Buffalo Ridge Trail #1151

Highlights: Famous waterfall, views, unusual lakes in a high mountain basin, easy access to a peak, and many opportunities for further exploration.

To Get There

Take Highway 14 to Walden and head north 9 miles on Highway 125 to the town of Cowdrey. Turn left (west) at the Cowdrey Store on CR 6W.

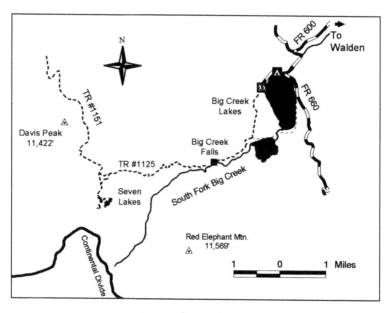

Seven Lakes Trail #1125

It soon turns to a gravel road, a bit washboardy but tolerable. Follow it as it curves around Independence Mountain. Before the old mining ghost town of Pearl, turn left at a sign to Big Creek Lake. This road will become FR 600. At Big Creek Lake, go straight at the fork, following a sign past the campground to the trailhead, which is well marked and has plenty of parking and restrooms. From Cowdrey to the trailhead is 22 miles, most of it gravel.

The Hike

The first 1.5 miles of this trail lead to Big Creek Falls, described in this book. This section of trail is part of an interpretive nature trail; brochures can be obtained at the trailhead. Some of the trail is boggy, and newly repaired wooden boardwalk traverses the wet spots. Because of the wetness, Trail #1125 isn't recommended for horse travel. Views

Three of the Seven Lakes with Red Elephant Mountain in the background

of Upper Big Creek Lake are a welcome surprise just before reaching the falls. The falls rush over a steep drop to a pool below under a dark, chilly forest. A foot path leads to the rock platform above the falls. The roar from up here is deafening, especially during summer runoff.

To continue on to Seven Lakes, continue past the falls, entering the Zirkel Wilderness as the path begins the climb along Big Creek. Your ascent will become increasingly strenuous as you encounter switchbacks up the wall of the gorge. Eventually, the trail breaks out onto terrific views of Upper Big Creek Lake, the elongated Independence Mountain, and the Sand Hills tucked up against the Medicine Bow Range. The trail steers across many wide marshy parks, typical of the north end of the Zirkel Wilderness because the region is lower in elevation than much of the rest of the wilderness area. When the trail finally reaches the top of the ridge, it ascends through forest of spruce, pine, and fir, then levels out before curving around into the basin. The intersection with the Davis Peak Trail is located on yet another large meadow. To reach the lakes, go left (south). To ascend Davis Peak, go right (north).

The name "Seven Lakes" reflects the official count of seven but is a misnomer. The basin is one large swampy spot with an ever-changing number of pools and lakes. Finding a dry, protected camping spot near the lakes can be tricky, especially if you visit early in the season. The largest and most lakelike lake (the others are barely more than glorified puddles) is the one closest to the foot of Red Elephant Mountain, which looms red-faced overhead to the south. If there are fish at Seven Lakes, they're in the large lake. At certain times of day, Seven Lakes seems to transport one into a Salvador Dali world, nothing but gray boulders and their motionless reflections in every direction.

To reach Davis Peak, retrace your steps to the trail fork and head up the meadow north. Davis Peak is visible ahead. Climb the flank of the mountain to a saddle between the mountain and the ridge. There is no proper trail up the talus slope to the summit. Be prepared with extra clothing layers for high winds and cold, threatening weather any time of year. The 0.25-mile climb up the mountainside is not unduly strenuous, but take into consideration the 11,422-foot elevation of the peak. You'll find remarkable views of the Zirkel Wilderness and the Sawtooth Range from the summit.

References

Aycock, Etholine, and Mary Hagen. *Larimer County Place Names: A History of Names on County Maps.* Fort Collins, CO: Old Army Press, 1984.

Bier, Edie. "History of Colorado State Forest." Unpublished manuscript.

Brown, Dee. *Bury My Heart at Wounded Knee.* New York: Bantam Books, 1970.

Case, Stanley R. *The Poudre.* Bellvue, CO: Stanley R. Case, 1995.

City and County of Fort Collins. Miscellaneous city and county open space brochures. Fort Collins, CO: City and County of Fort Collins, various years. Available at city and county offices, public libraries, and trailheads.

Crum, Sally. *People of the Red Earth: American Indians of Colorado.* Santa Fe: Ancient City Press, 1996.

Eichler, Geo. R. *Colorado Place Names.* Boulder, CO: Johnson Publishing Co., 1977.

Evans, Howard Ensign, and Mary Alice Evans. *Cache la Poudre.* Niwot, CO: University Press of Colorado, 1991.

Gray, John S., Charlene Trisner, Jere Paulmeno, Frank Hall, and Stephanie A. Grillos. *The Poudre River.* Fort Collins, CO: Gro-Pub Group, 1976.

Gresham, Hazel. *North Park.* Cheyenne: Pioneer Printing, 1975.

Hagen, Mary. *Hiking Trails of Northern Colorado.* Fort Collins, CO: Azure Publishing, 1994.

Hughes, J. Donald. *American Indians in Colorado.* Boulder, CO: Pruett Publishing, 1977.

Lischka, Joseph J., Mark E. Miller, R. Branson Reynolds, Dennis Dahms, Kathy Joyner-McGuire, and David McGuire. *An Archaeological Inventory in North Park*. Denver: Bureau of Land Management, 1983.

Marsh, Charles S. *People of the Shining Mountains*. Boulder, CO: Pruett Publishing, 1982.

Swanson, Evadene Burris. *Fort Collins Yesterdays*. Fort Collins, CO: Don-Art Printers, 1975.

Tremblay, William. *The June Rise: The Apocryphal Letters of Joseph Antoine Janis*. Logan: Utah State University Press, 1994.

U.S. Forest Service. *History of Routt National Forest*. 2d ed. U.S. Forest Service, 1972.

Walters, Hildred, and Lorraine Young. *Colorado Prairie Tales*. Scottsbluff, NE: Business Farmers Printing Co., 1974.

Ward, Louisa Arps, and Elinor Eppich Kingery. *High-Country Names*. Colorado Mountain Club, 1966.

Watrous, Ansel. *History of Larimer County*. Fort Collins, CO: Vestige Press, 1911.

INDEX

References to hikes described in this book are printed in **boldface type.**

Printed in the USA
CPSIA information can be obtained
at www.ICGtesting.com
JSHW012021140824
68134JS00033B/2817